Jamaica in the 21st Century

Revisiting the First Decade

Livingstone Thompson

WITH AN ESSAY BY PETAL THOMPSON-WILLIAMS

University Press of America,® Inc.
Lanham • Boulder • New York • Toronto • Plymouth, UK

Copyright © 2017 by University Press of America,® Inc.
4501 Forbes Boulevard, Suite 200, Lanham, Maryland 20706
UPA Acquisitions Department (301) 459-3366

Unit A, Whitacre Mews, 26-34 Stannary Street,
London SE11 4AB, United Kingdom

All rights reserved
Printed in the United States of America
British Library Cataloguing in Publication Information Available

Library of Congress Control Number: 2016933950
ISBN: 978-0-7618-6751-7 (pbk : alk. paper)—ISBN: 978-0-7618-6752-4 (electronic)

∞™ The paper used in this publication meets the minimum requirements of American National Standard for Information Sciences Permanence of Paper for Printed Library Materials, ANSI/NISO Z39.48-1992.

Dedicated to the late Rev. Dr Robert W. M. Cuthbert

Dr Robert W. M. Cuthbert was President of the Executive Board of
the Moravian Church in Jamaica (1981–1985) and Founder of
Unitas of Jamaica Ltd and Christian Action for Development (CADEC).
Dr Cuthbert was shot and killed on February 24, 1985,
but his killers have never been brought to justice.
The failure to find and charge the perpetrators of this crime
is symptomatic of law and order in Jamaica,
where murderers kill with impunity.
In that sense Cuthbert's death calls to mind the many who have died
but for whose family justice has not been realised.
Crime in Jamaica is a major challenge to be overcome
but other challenges are to be found in the chapters of this publication.

Contents

Acknowledgments	ix
Introduction	xi
Responding to National Issues	xii
Dedication	xiii
Relevance	xiv
Omission	xiv
Audience	xvi
1 National Issues and Policies	1
UWI Trends and Policy Needs, September 7, 2003	1
The Terrorism Prevention Act 2003, November 11, 2003	3
A Sterile Budget Debate, May 2, 2004	6
Why the Fascination with Gambling? June 6, 2004	7
The Church, Party Leadership and Unity, July 4, 2004	10
Teachers Need Inspiration, September 5, 2004	12
Whose Victory Is This? February 6, 2005	14
A Blow to Political Bigotry, February 9, 2005	16
Ras Noah and the Hawk: Making Fun of God, May 1, 2005	17
And There Shall Be Rain! April 3, 2005	19
Dawn Ritch and the Educated Class, July 3, 2005	21
Independence and Development, August 7, 2005	23
The Ethics of Funding Education, September 4, 2005	26
Is Hanging the Answer to Crime? November 6, 2005	28
Education of Persons with Disability, December 4, 2005	30
The Duppy Economic Policy, May 7, 2006	32
Implications of Independence, August 6, 2006	34

	New Electoral Commission: Cosmetic Change Only?	
	December 3, 2006	36
	Crime and Divine Intervention, January 7, 2007	38
2	Regional and International Issues	41
	Religion on the Caribbean Agenda, July 6, 2003	41
	CARICOM, the UN and Moral/Ethical Principles, March 7, 2004	43
	A Crisis in Human Sexuality, December 5, 2004	45
	The Death of Thousands: A Theological Problem, January 1, 2005	47
	The Church and Human Sexuality, March 6, 2005	49
	Long Live the IRA, October 2, 2005	51
	Sexual Relations, Rape, and Civil Unions, June 4, 2006	53
	Economic Success and Religious Affiliation, September 3, 2006	55
	Apartheid Is Dead, Not Its Children, November 5, 2006	57
	Cricket World Cup: Priced beyond the Ordinary, February 4, 2007	59
	Migrating to Ireland: Pull Factors and Limitations, April 1, 2007	61
3	Faith and the Church	65
	The Church's Influence on Emancipation, August 3, 2003	65
	Interfaith Relations, October 5, 2003	67
	Knowledge-based Economy and the Church, January 2, 2004	69
	The First Protestant Denomination in Jamaica: Its Advent and Character, December 8, 2004	71
	Moravians in Wider Society, March 31, 2005	74
	The Bishops of Rome and the Anti-Popes, April 8, 2005	75
	Happy New Year My Foot! January 1, 2006	79
	In the Beginning, God, April 2, 2006	81
	A Female Primate to the Rescue? July 2, 2006	83
	Dr. Lewin Williams and Caribbean Theology, October 1, 2006	85
	A Significant Church Milestone, March 4, 2007	87
	Religions and Economic Success, June 2014	89
4	Letters to the Editor	95
	Comments on Religious Articles, December 21, 1990	95
	Early Role of the Moravians, January 17, 1991	96
	A Comment on C. Reynolds' Plea for "Sense," November 12, 1998	97
	Re-interpreting Christian Tradition and History	99
	Moravian Position on Homosexuality, November 2, 2003	100
	Ganja Case Not Strong Enough, December 27, 2003	101
	Why the JLP Is Wary of the Social Partnership, January 23, 2004	104
	The Murder of Rev Dr RWM Cuthbert, February 29, 2004	105
	Reconsidering the Rights Law, March 3, 2006	105

Postscript: Jamaica's Programme of Advancement through Health
    and Education   107
  Petal Thompson-Williams, M.Ed (UTech)
    Introduction   107
    Health   108
    Education   108
    The Future   109

Bibliography   111

Acknowledgments

The articles in this publication, with the exception of the postscript, were first published in the *Gleaner* at different times over a number of years. They were collated for the purposes of this publication. We thank the Gleaner Company for the permission to reproduce the articles here.

Introduction

This book is a sort of socio-historical enterprise because it unearths and retrieves a series of critiques and commentaries published in the Jamaica Daily Gleaner and the Sunday Gleaner during the first decade of 21st century Jamaica. The author revisits his time as a guest columnist of the Sunday Gleaner in Jamaica, a position that gives one the privilege of being at the forefront of public social commentary. The fact that the newspaper has a combined hardcopy sales and online readership of over 750,000, puts the newspaper in a privileged position to influence public opinion. As a leading regional newspaper, the Sunday paper, together with other daily versions published by the Gleaner Company, has the enviable position of being the foremost medium of public discourse. This book then is a selection and a snapshot of 21st century discourse in Jamaica.

The editorial decision for a guest columnist is clearly not an exact science. In my own case it came about that I was approached by the Associate Editor at the time, Colin Steer, who asked whether I would write a monthly column for the paper, on any issue. This was somewhat fortuitous in that I seemed to come to the attention of the editorial team after I wrote a letter to the Editor in response to an article by C. Roy Reynolds, one of its leading journalists at the time. Reynolds had written that it was illogical for people to give thanks that Jamaica was spared the ravages of hurricane Mitch, which wreaked havoc in the region, when it passed through just at the end of the Hurricane Season, in November 1998. In my response to Reynolds I tried to tackle the dilemma of people thanking God for being spared the worst effects of an event in which others suffered badly. That wasn't the last time that I tried, in a newspaper article, to come to terms with this issue. About six years later, after the Christmas 2004 Tsunami that killed over 250,000 persons in and around Indonesia, I picked up this issue again. In the response to Reynolds I suggested that, in an event of being spared, one has three possible responses: either to be sad at being spared, disregard the fact that one is spared or rejoice for being spared. The person of faith ends with the most difficult choice because, in choosing to give thanks to God, they then have the challenge of giving account for being thankful. This was what Reynolds called illogical. There were other articles in the newspaper later that month that commented on Reynolds' column, as well as my response. It was not the first time I had written to the editor but it was in the wake of the letter that I was asked, by the Associate Editor, to make further regular comments on issues in society.

RESPONDING TO NATIONAL ISSUES

Writing in response to what someone else has written is fairly easy because the focus of the response is already determined. The only challenge is what to say on the subject matter. However, when the agenda has not been set, it is a little more difficult, as one must not only determine the focus but also the angle. Happily for me and other columnists, the subjects for commentaries were often determined by local and international events. There was no shortage of issues beckoning comment, whether issues related to crime, education, political parties, or government economic policies, at local level, or similar issues at regional and international levels. Columnists in general tried to focus comments on issues of the day. Since articles were expected to be submitted the Thursday before the Sunday when it would appear in the press, we could wait until Wednesday night to see the leading issues that were trending that called for comment. For that reason the editor would often have several columnists giving a different angle on the same issue, even though there was no agreement beforehand.

The socio-economic challenges for Jamaica at the turn of the century were dominated by issues related to the economy, crime and violence and how policies of government and the activities of the civil society, including the church, responded to them. For that reason community capacity building, unemployment and youth impact would feature significantly in commentaries. The role of columnists like me was to critique the policies, or lack thereof, and in the process generate public conversation. In fact the idea for this book arose after revisiting one of those articles relating to crime and violence. I was browsing the internet towards the end of 2014 and came upon a few articles I wrote for the Gleaner between 2003 and 2007. I had forgotten about some of these and so started looking for others that I might also have forgotten. I read with interest those that I found on several societal issues and started questioning whether things have really changed in Jamaica. One article, "Crime and Divine Intervention," which was published in 2007, I sent to my brother who held an advisory position in one of the government ministries and asked whether he thought it was still relevant. For his answer he copied me in an email he sent to two ministers of government, suggesting that they read the article again, as they would find it interesting, in light of issues they had recently spoken about in their respective ministries. This is where the idea for *Jamaica in the 21 st Century* was born. The underlying question it poses is whether there might be value and if so, what relevance, if I were to unearth the articles buried under pages of the years. This book then is a selective archaeological enterprise, designed to aid memory and, if possible, to help us avoid reinventing the wheel. Many of the issues that preoccupy us in this decade are issues that have been addressed before. It might be of use to familiarise ourselves with the earlier discussion.

DEDICATION

In a sense, then, the challenges during the first decade of the 21st century were not different from those at the end of the 20th century. The issue of crime and violence, for example, has not gone away. Today it is considered to be an improvement if, in a single calendar year, less than 1000 people are killed in violent crimes. Although the year 1979 is three and a half decades ago, it is still active in our memories because in that year violent deaths breached the 900 per year mark. It was clear then that we were in a new era. We ought not to speak on this subject without thinking of the hundreds who lost their lives and to dedicate this work to them. We do not confine our sorrow to the families of the last decade only but all families who bear the scar of loss due to violence. One of those families is that of the late Rev Dr Robert W M Cuthbert who, at the time he was killed on February 24, 1985, was president of the Provincial Elders' Conference (PEC), the executive board of Moravian Church. This work is dedicated to him because he symbolises the church engaging in public discourse.

Cuthbert was a leading cleric of Jamaica and the Caribbean region and was instrumental in initiating several projects, for example CADEC (Christian Action for Development), JEMM (Jamaica Ecumenical Mutual Mission) and Unitas of Jamaica, all of which reflected the theme of development that was, and still is, a feature of Caribbean theology. When compared with the other-worldly emphases in received European theologies that formed the historical Protestant Churches in the region, Caribbean theology was decidedly this-worldly. It is a political theology that emerged in the decade after regional political independence and for that reason had the shaping of a distinctive Caribbean identity as part of its project. Through his involvement in the Caribbean Conference of Churches, the Eastern West Indies Province of the Moravian Church and the Moravian Church in Jamaica, Cuthbert demonstrated himself as a visionary leader. His term as president of the PEC was one of the shortest (1981-1985), but his leadership influences are still evident in Jamaica, the Eastern Caribbean and the United States because his theological mentees are leaders of churches and educational institutions in these locations.

RELEVANCE

At a deeper level, however, the book throws up theological analyses of a variety of questions raised and discussed in the Jamaica during the 1st decade of the 21st century. The presence of a strong theological critique of societal issues should not surprise anyone, given the prominence of religion in Jamaica's social life. Issues of religion gleam through the political rhetoric and are ever present in the reggae songs for which the island is known. Therefore, the social, political and economic issues raised in public discourse could not be fully addressed without taking cognizance of a religious view point. This author is one of many commentators who, although not claiming to be speaking on behalf of a particular religious community, were quite comfortable in the religious lenses through which they gaze on the social space and were never keen to distance themselves from the religious community to which they belong.

Although the views expressed here represent a snapshot in time, it will become clear as we read and re-read these commentaries that not only do some of the questions remain to be settled but also that these opinions remain relevant in current debate. This is true whether we speak of gambling, crime or human sexuality. The debates on many issues have moved forward, for example education policy, the shape of the economy, homosexuality and the leadership in churches and political parties. However, the commentaries are still an important historical reference point. In the new formulations of public debate it might be important to remind ourselves of grounds that we have already covered.

OMISSION

A publication of this nature runs the risk of being charged with omission because when looking through a small window, at a particular point in time, one is bound to overlook some issues. One obvious omission from commentary is the tourism sector, which has for years been the main foreign exchange earner for the local economy. One could argue that the sector was implicated in commentaries about gambling, which has remained a major fascination for some tourism spokesperson. It is also true that issues relating to crime have had a bearing on the tourism industry, which has seen some jitters after visitors to the island have been murdered, or when tourists die in questionable or tragic circumstances. The truth though is that the goose laying the golden eggs, which tourism is, has remained relatively stable and is a significant predictor of growth in the coming period.

A commentary on tourism at this time would need to focus attention on the importance of the industry paying attention to the cultural awareness training of staff. Issues relating to culture are mentioned at entry level training for staff but primarily in the sense of staff being able to communicate and explain local culture. However, there is another area of cultural awareness training, which relates to understanding the norms and values of other cultures. In the way we offer service and the products we develop we must be cognisant of those cultural norms and values. Considering the variety of cultures, American, European, Latin American, Asian, to name a few, from which we receive visitors, understanding the cultural norms and assumptions for these should be treated as an imperative. Staff at all levels of the tourism industry need to become culturally proficient, which mean having the relevant attitude and developing the knowledge and skills needed to respond appropriately to people of different cultures.

The tendency of destinations in the region to promote local cultures in an exclusive way might in fact indicate a sort of cultural blindness. That is where one's culture is lifted above others and the need to develop knowledge and the need to make appropriate changes to one's behaviour, in light of other cultures, are minimised. In a webinar on cultural awareness, which was delivered to tourism managers in the region, one executive gave feedback that the facilitator's voice was not what she was accustomed to hearing. In response the facilitator used it as an example to explain cultural blindness, which assumes that one's own cultural assumptions and expectations set the standard for other cultures. The inclination to deny the need for cultural training or the tendency to minimise cultural differences or to universalise one's own cultural habits, also indicates the same cultural blindness or ethnocentrism.

The need for managers to move towards cultural proficiency is not unique to Jamaica or to the Caribbean region. In a 2014 research, which was carried out by Living Cultural Solutions Ltd, it was revealed that 75% of managers and 80% of staff in Dublin hotels had had no cultural awareness training at all. Considering the nature of the industry and the need to take advantage of new markets, this is, to say the least, sobering. The good thing, however, is that both the Tourism Product Development Company (TPDCo), the Jamaica Hotels and Tourist Association (JHTA) and Caribbean Tourism Organisation (CTO) are aware of this training deficit. The will to break new training ground and lack of funds are cited as constraining factors. Tourism organisations are far too dependent on government and must be challenged to put some of their profits into training and brand development.

AUDIENCE

The fact that the issues discussed in this book affect the lives of most individuals in Jamaican society, one can say that the book is meant for the whole public, as did the broadsheet in which the articles appeared. However, one imagines that it will be of particular interest to students, social entrepreneurs and emerging leaders in church, community and government, as well as non-government organisations. Treading as it does through thorny moral-ethical questions, the book may be seen as a practitioner's guide to public debate in 21st century Jamaica.

The book is divided into five sections, with the articles and in each section appearing in the chronological order in which they were published in the Gleaner. The absence of footnotes reflects the original way in which the articles were published. However, there is a bibliography for the references to publications that have been made. By keeping the dates for each article, the reader will get a sense of the historical sequence in which issues arose and received comment. This sequence, therefore, is not so much about the development of thought as it is about the issues as they appeared to be relevant at the time. Section 1 is focussed on national issues and policies, Section 2 deals with regional and international issues, while Section 3 is dedicated to issues about faith and the church. Section 4 is comprised of letters written to the editor between 1991 and 2006. This section includes the letter written in response to C Roy Reynolds, which was the genesis of writing regularly for the newspaper. The Postscript is a brief comment of the contemporary situation in Jamaica. In this essay and using the framework of Jamaica's Programme of Advancement through Health and Education (PATH), Petal Thompson-Williams offers an analysis of issues being faced by Jamaican society in the second decade of the 21st century.

The author takes full responsibility for any error or omission in the publication. However, for the support of this publication I want to thank Sheree Rhoden of the Gleaner Company and former employees Colin Steer and Warren Wint. Thanks also to Delwen Giles for reading the entire manuscript. Finally, thanks to my family, especially my wife Jean-Marie, who had to put up with the dynamics of me pursuing another publication.

Livingstone Thompson
January 2016

Chapter One

National Issues and Policies

UWI TRENDS AND POLICY NEEDS,
SEPTEMBER 7, 2003

At the beginning of another academic year it may serve us well to consider the recent data in the 2001 official statistics of the University of the West Indies (UWI). A number of very interesting features can be discerned, which have a bearing on the educational policy, philosophy and programmes of the participating countries. The first relates to the overall numbers of students registered. The overall population of the university has moved from a mere 33 persons (23 males and 10 females) in 1948/49 to well over 19,000 today. The growth of the population in Trinidad has been the most significant. While there were 910 students at Mona in 1960/1 there were only 67 students at St. Augustine. However, by 1980/81 the population at Mona it was 4,579 while St. Augustine's had grown to 2,913. Today, the largest campus is Mona, which in 2000/01 had 8,758 students, followed by St. Augustine in Trinidad with 6.967 and Cave Hill in Barbados with 3,740. In each case, the host country provides the bulk of the student population. This means that Barbados, with a population of about 270,000 has a university registration of about 14 students for every 1000 residents. Trinidad and Tobago, with 1.3 million people, has nearly five per 1000. When we factor in the other two universities in Jamaica, (University of Technology 6,733 and Northern Caribbean University 4,500) with a population of 2.5 million, Jamaica has about eight persons registered in university per 1000 residents.

Interesting Feature

Another interesting feature is the shift in numbers of female students being registered. Up to 1981/82 there were more males than females but female student registration was always increasing at a faster rate. The turning point was 1982/83 when for the first time the overall number of females surpassed the number of males. From a total of 4,869 female students among the three campuses in 1982/83, the female population moved in 2000/01 to 12,660. During that same period the male population moved from 4,704 to 6,805. In other words, 65 per cent of the university's population at 2000/01 was female and 35 per cent male. Where the female population has grown by 160 per cent in the last 20 years, the male population has grown by about 45 per cent. The increasing female registration of fulltime students can be seen on all three campuses. At the end of 2000/01 females accounted for 69 per cent of the student population at Mona, 67 per cent at Cave Hill and 57 per cent at St. Augustine. For students in the part-time programmes, the percentages for females are higher for all three campuses. For full-time students at the undergraduate level, Mona showed 70 per cent female, 68 per cent at Cave Hill and 56 per cent at St. Augustine. At the level of higher degrees, females account for 62 per cent al Mona, 61 per cent at Cave Hill and 59 per cent at St. Augustine.

A third feature of the Official Statistics is that for the first time in the history of the university, the year 2000/01 showed an overall decrease in registration over the previous year. The registration at St. Augustine has always showed an increase on the previous years, which means that Cave Hill and Mona account for that decrease. St Augustine, in fact, had an overall increase of 107. Cave Hill showed a decrease in registration in 1966/67 and 1992/93. Mona showed decreases on the previous years in 1985/86, 1986/87 and 1999/2000. The most recent decreases in registration at Mona may be due to the other options for pursuing degrees that are currently available in Jamaica. It will be interesting to see whether this trend will continue.

A fourth feature of interest is part-time registration. At Mona, only in faculties of law and the medical sciences are there no part-time students at the undergraduate, diploma or certificate levels. Naturally, there are particularities relating to the nature of these programmes that may account for this. However, one wonders whether this is also evidence of the elitism of a former dispensation that we continue to see in these faculties. At the same time, 43 per cent of the students registered in the social sciences faculty in 2000/01 and 33 per cent in arts and education were part-time student. When all the faculties are considered, 36 per cent of student registration in 2000/01 was part-time. The growing number of part-time students may also be a factor that has facilitated the increased registration of women.

A fifth feature relates to the higher degrees awarded by the university. There is clearly a trend towards the social sciences, where 61 per cent of the all degrees granted by Mona in 2000/01was in this area. (84 per cent of those receiving degrees were Jamaicans.) In the case of Cave Hill, the figure was 50 per cent and 35 per cent in the case of St. Augustine. There is need to understand properly the meaning of this trend because they have a bearing on development.

From the above assessment it is clear that Jamaica must take stock of the levels of registration in general and registration of males in particular. However, the area that concerns this writer most critically is the granting of higher degrees, which indicates where advanced research is taking place and where we are building our capacities to break new ground for industry.

Social Sciences

One wonders about the extent to which research in the social sciences will eventually have an impact on the growth and development of our economy and the extent to which such research is enabling us to add value to our products. The predisposition of persons to opt for advanced research in the social sciences seems to be a consequence of traditional attitudes in education, rather than to any careful assessment of what the long term developmental needs of the society may be. For Jamaica, this issue is important because 63 per cent of all degrees granted to Jamaicans at the higher level in 2001 were in the social sciences. This trend is quite understandable given the deep social problems we are experiencing in terms of crime and social dislocation. However, with a long tradition of involvement in mining and agriculture, where there is a greater capacity for developing value-added products, it is a pity that Mona is not making the engineering and agricultural sciences more available to Jamaicans. There is increasing difficulty for Jamaican students to go to Trinidad & Tobago or Barbados where we have faculties in engineering and agriculture. The University of the West Indies at Mona must address this question of programmes on offer to the long-term developmental needs of the Jamaican society. The administration at Mona must therefore think again about the long-term developmental meaning and implications of this predisposition to the social sciences at the level of higher degrees.

THE TERRORISM PREVENTION ACT 2003, NOVEMBER 11, 2003

Prime Minister P. J. Patterson has said he would like to see the Terrorism Prevention Act, 2003 fully promulgated by March 2004, so that Jamaica would be seen by the United Nations to be co-operating with the measures to prevent terrorism. In this article I want to look at some aspects of the Act.

The Meaning of Terrorism

A fundamental assertion in the 79 page Act is that a terrorist act must have a political, religious or ideological objective, which is directed at: (a) Intimidating the public, or a segment of the public, with regard to its security including its economic security; or (b) compelling a person, a government, a domestic or an international organization to do or to refrain from doing any act, whether the person, government or organisation is inside or outside Jamaica.

The intimidation or compulsion may be an act or an omission, which being intentionally committed (i) results in the death or serious bodily harm to the individual, (ii) endangers a person's life, (iii) causes substantial damage to public or private property, (iv) causes serious interference or disruption of public or private essential services.

The difficulty with the idea of intimidating the public or a segment of the public is the question of what is meant. The most intimidating conduct that I have witnessed by a group of persons is the conduct of party supporters travelling in a political motorcade during a general election campaign. Although I only heard of the damage to property, I certainly felt that my life and the lives of people in the buses were endangered. Could I appeal to the provisions of this Act for the persons to be charged with terrorism or would a number of persons like me have to testify to having been endangered? Clearly, supporters of a political party intentionally carried out the conduct. This interpretation is not mitigated by the fact that the Act attempts to make a distinction between an act of terrorism and lawful advocacy, protest, dissent or stoppage of work, which do not involve activities intended to result in the situations referred to in the paragraph above. However, the Government will want to look again at this aspect of the bill, which is part of what is being perceived as an attempt to stifle legitimate protest. Mind you, I am delighted by the fact that the burning of tyres and the blocking of roads and the wilful destruction of property by mobs are now to be construed as acts of terrorism. I have never been able to appreciate the logic of those actions.

Terrorism and the Security Forces

There is an effort in the Act to ensure that armed conflicts or actions of the military or state, which conform to rules governing international law, are not construed as acts of terrorism. Nevertheless, given the propensity of our security forces to become engaged in questionable activities, the challenge they will have under this Act is to show that that they are not acting as terrorists. If the unlawful acts of intimidation, the endangerment of life and the destruction of property, which are believed to be part of the modus operandi of the police, can be shown to have an ideological or political motive, they could face a charge of terrorism. I am sure Mr. Wilmot Perkins will be happy for this provision because he has been asserting that certain actions of the police are outside the boundaries of international law. The Act seems to allow that he could make a case for terrorism against the police.

Terrorist by Association

In making a determination of whether an accused has participated in a terrorist act, the Act allows the Supreme Court to consider a number of things, including usage of names, symbols and other things that can be associated with a group. However, it is possible under the present provision of the Act for an individual to be charged with facilitating an act of terrorism, "whether or not the accused knows the identity of any of the persons who constitute the terrorist group." Evidently, it is imagined that it is possible for someone to be in collusion with a person or persons with terrorist intent, without having an idea of whom the partners in the crime are. Under the proposal, the Supreme Court will not need to demonstrate that the accused has any knowledge of the personalities involved in the terrorist act. Here again the Government may want to revisit the bill because it seems unreasonable to link someone with perpetration of an act of terror, if in the mind of the individual the personalities behind a terror group are neither known to them nor known to exist. Provisions similar to this in the laws in England and the United States make for significant violation of human rights. The Government of Jamaica is not under any compulsion to follow those countries down that road.

The Right of Concealment

The Act allows for two instances in which information relating to a terrorist offence may be concealed from a constable. One is where it can be shown that the individual had reasonable grounds for not making the disclosure. This would include, for example, a situation where in the course of his or her duty in the bank an employee gets a sense that a terrorist act is about to be committed but rather than reporting it to the police reports it to a senior bank official, providing that this is the procedure established by the bank for reporting such matters. The other instance is where an attorney-at-law receives information in preparing to make a defence for a client who may be accused of a terrorist offence. It is important for priests and pastors to know that under the present draft, they are not immune from prosecution if they are known to have information relating to terrorism as it is described in the Draft. The pastor or priest can be charged as terrorist by omission for failing to disclose to the police in a reasonable time, information that may have a bearing on terrorist activity. There is in fact a de facto presumption of suspicion of the role that a pastor or priest may play in the normal course of their duties. The onus on the lawmakers in this country is to ensure that the Terrorism Prevention Act cannot be abused on political, religious or ideological grounds. Unfortunately, that guarantee seems to be lacking in its present form. Therefore, a careful revision of the proposals seems to be an imperative.

A STERILE BUDGET DEBATE, MAY 2, 2004

The Government must take responsibility for allowing its presentations in the Budget Debate to be overshadowed by the issue of the exchange rate regime, which was raised by the Leader of the Opposition. The Opposition Leader seemed to have stepped into a vacuum created by the failure of the Government to articulate with clarity, coherence and conviction, the economic direction in which the country is headed, and the rationale for the direction. So, as we speak, we do not know the main features of the Government's economic policy, nor are we aware of the political philosophy on which they are based. But we need to know. The unfortunate thing about the discussion on the exchange rate is not just that it is speculative but, more importantly, it is happening in a manner that excludes the average Jamaican. It is good to know that academic studies have been done on this matter, as indeed on a host of other economic issues. It's also great to know that our leaders read these studies. However, I am not sure of the value of imposing the technicalities on the unlearned. With the proposition that the fixed exchange rate is far more effective, we have to assume that those who do not pursue this model are either dumb or do not want their economy to do well. This is so preposterous! I am alarmed at the way in which it has been seized upon, especially on the Breakfast Club, as if we are hearing, 'for the first time at last,' the sole gospel for our economic salvation. The discussion has become alienating and sterile.

Economic Model

If we are not careful, the Budget this year could be seen to revolve around issues with which the people are not familiar, or with which they cannot immediately identify. It may well be that Hugh Small does not compare with the Davies' and the Seagas, as a Finance Minister. I do not have the competence to judge him. However, one of the things I recall was the clarity of his presentations and his attempt to make clear the basic outline of the economic model his Government was pursuing. One did not have to agree with it, but at least one heard the position with clarity. In these days, we are long on information and counter-information but short on clarity of political philosophy and economic model.

The point, then, is that the Government should be clear about what it wishes to do and present it in a way that people can share the vision. One of the weaknesses of this generation of political leaders is their lack of conviction and, consequently, their inability to motivate. It is not enough that we must wait for the time of general election to see attempts to capture the interest of the public.

Lack of Clarity

One way in which the lack of clarity expresses itself is in the area of education. We have heard a lot of talk about the amount of funds the education sector is getting, but we do not have clarity about the main educational priorities. Churches like the Moravian Church, which have been involved in education since 1823, and which remain committed to education for social and economic transformation, are stake-holders in education. However, we do not know what the Government wants to accomplish in the next five or so years and how we can be a part of it. What we see is a measure of suffocation because the Government cannot finance certain programmes. Even with that, however, it is not abundantly clear what the Government wants to achieve with the limited resources it has to spend.

Another evidence of lack of clarity in Government is the desire to move the country in different directions at the same time. We have heard a lot of talk about values, attitudes and work ethic, as indeed we have heard about the need to expand the gambling industry. The Government wants the church to be its partner in helping to fashion a society, the core values of which will guarantee our well-being and prosperity. However, the Government is insistent on the expansion of gambling, as part of its economic strategy, which is most surely counter-productive to its interest in the creation of a sustainable economy. Gambling is of no benefit to the masses of the nation. It transfers money from the poor to those who are more financially secure. Gambling is a bad habit of people who have money to throw away. It is the panacea that the Government falls on when they lust after quick money but has no idea of how to create wealth in a sustainable way. The Government, which prides itself in the inculcation of high values, should be ashamed for allowing the country to be overrun by this blight. This is yet again evidence that the Government needs to think further on its economic policies. The recent debates in the House of Representative were conducted as if those on one side of the House are simply addressing people on the other side. They show the need to score points and to prove that the other side has faulted. The point of the debates is not to communicate to voters—in any case, fewer and fewer people seem to tune in to listen. Now that the debate in the House has ended, so to speak, I hope that the conversation with the masses will begin.

WHY THE FASCINATION WITH GAMBLING?
JUNE 6, 2004

The Government and leaders in the private sector, especially tourism, are well aware of the wider Christian community's opposition to gambling. They also know that the onus is on them to make the case for the further expansion of the gambling industry because it is not immediately evident that the economic gains of gambling will outweigh the social costs. Those who believe there is much to be gained from expansion may want to show the extent to which the gambling industry, in its current stratification, is making a meaningful contribution to the GDP of the country. They must also answer the question of who the beneficiaries of the Lucky 5, Catch 3 and the lottery etc., are and show this in terms of the improved income by those who participate in these gambling activities on a daily basis.

Unconvincing Argument

There are two reasons why the case for gambling and its continued expansion, especially into the area of casinos, is not convincing. The first is that the pro-gamblers have not yet been able to debunk the traditional association of gambling with poor work ethic, violence, money laundering, negative impact on families and low ethical and moral values. The opposition of the Christian community did not exist before gambling came into being, so that it can be said to be completely based on suspicion or prejudice. It was because Christians came to see deterioration in family and communal life as a result of the ethic attitude that underlies gambling. The converse was also seen—that the deterioration of ethical and moral values in the community and families went hand in hand with the lure of gambling. The hesitation of the Government to immediately throw its full weight behind gambling expansion is not due to pressure from the churches, as many people seem to think. Rather, the leaders of Government themselves are not convinced that gambling is a wonderful idea, let alone a panacea, to solve our economic woes in a sustained way. So, despite the figure from Robert Buddhan of the University of the West Indies and others, the case has simply not been made convincingly beyond doubt. The fascination with gambling in general, and casino gambling in particular, is simply evidence of the short-sightedness and desire for instant but unsustainable economic gratification that exists in a capitalist mind-set. The second reason why the case for gambling and its expansion is not convincing is that, even with the impressive figures of economic benefit, the argument is constructed on a foundation that is questionable.

According to Godfrey Dyer of the Jamaica and Hotel and Tourism Association, Beverly Lopez of the Private Sector Organisation of Jamaica and Dr. Kenny Anthony of St. Lucia, casino gambling will improve the tourism product. I believe they mean by this, that more tourists will be attracted to our shores and spend more money if we offer them the option of casinos. I am no expert on tourism but that does not sound to me like improvement in a product, although it does reflect a strategy to improve arrivals. It was the same argument about improving the tourism product that was used for the expansion of the prostitution industry in Thailand. It was argued that the American and European tourists would come in droves only if there were an unending supply of girls from which they could pick and choose for their pleasure and fancy. The prostitution industry in Thailand expanded; there were improved arrivals but all these came at a great cost to the social and health sectors. The main beneficiaries were the corrupt persons involved in human trade, who subjected the young .women to the most inhumane treatment for the benefit of the visitor. Neither the girls, nor their families, nor the society at large has had any positive outcome of which they could be proud.

A Myth

What is being proposed as improvement of the tourism product is nothing more than a series of self-serving gimmicks to lure a certain constituency. That constituency, which is believed to be interested in casino gambling, may also be interested in drugs, prostitution and other societal ills. If they want these, why do we not make them available too? I am not sure, however, that the gambling-loving constituency is the largest constituency of possible visitors to the island.

The tourism leaders may be operating under a myth not dissimilar to pub owners in Ireland, who believed it was not possible for non-smoking pubs to do well. These pub owners tried stoutly to resist the ban on smoking in all places of work, which the Irish Government instituted on March 29, 2004. Their fear, arising from the myth, was that the pub industry would go into recession. However, the transition to a smoke-free workplace has not only gone smoothly but has also shown improved income for owners, as they are able now to cater to non-smokers, who formerly would not venture into the heavily-smoked pub atmosphere. The Government considered that the likely fall in GDP as a result of the absence of smoke in the workplace, cannot be compared with the long-term benefit expected to accrue from the reduction of the cost of treating smoke-related illnesses. The move was not only wise from a health point of view but also proved to be a prudent economic and fiscal decision.

Looking for Alternatives

It would seem that the tourism leadership, as well as the pro-gamblers in the Government, do not want to broaden the span of their vision and look for other alternatives for the development of tourism. The fascination with casino gambling is approaching the point of fanaticism. Are we to understand that there are no tourists anywhere in the world who would be prepared to spend money to see more of Jamaica's heritage, community life, wildlife, flora and fauna?

As one respected economist suggested recently, the capitalists in Jamaica are interested more in buying and selling than in investment for sustained economic growth. It could be that the ease with which money can enter and leave the gambling industry, is driving the fanatical interest of that industry. We are evidently in a dispensation where the political and business leadership is so focused on immediate gains for housekeeping purposes that it is unable to delay its desire for instant gratification.

THE CHURCH, PARTY LEADERSHIP AND UNITY, JULY 4, 2004

Both the People's National Party and the Jamaica Labour Party are going through a process of leadership change. This process would have been completed and, hopefully, the question of succession would have eventually been settled by the time we get within a few months of the next general election. From the point of view of the Christian community, the issue of who is chosen to lead the main political parties is important because of the impact that the leader, who may well become the Prime Minister, can have on the spiritual, moral and ethical life of the country. The way the discussion about potential leaders is taking place in the public media, especially on the talk shows, would give the impression that the views of persons, who speak from the point of view of the religious .community on this issue, are not important. It also true, though, that the leaders of churches do not wish to appear partisan and prefer not to get drawn up into useless speculations just for the sake of talk. Nevertheless, the question of the leadership of the political parties is one to which the Christian community also pays close attention.

It is a real possibility that if the Christian community were to become united in its support for a particular candidate or a particular party, there is a good chance that that person or party would come out in front because the Christian community is probably the single largest community in Jamaica. It is not likely though, that unity will develop around this issue, because the church is too aware of weakness and folly of political leadership and would not sacrifice or limit its freedom to openly criticise any leader by giving him or her unqualified endorsement.

Church and Political Influence

In countries such as the United States, Greece, Sweden, South Africa and even Australia, the Christian churches play a significant role in influencing political life and the formation of governments. This influence is not only related to the unity of the Christian community in those countries but also to their strident political views. The leadership of the Jamaican church is keenly aware of the inherent divisiveness in our politics and the ease with which political zeal gets translated into political violence. The leaders of the churches fear that the desire for victory and the temptation for power among political rivals have for too long been at the expense of peace.

The rhetoric of their public conversations, and then regular tirades in Parliament by political representatives, communicate the idea that the political opponent is an enemy to be defeated rather than a rival whose support is to be won. From the period of the 1970s to the most recent General Elections, one of the things the church has emphasised is that persons contending for political office should be much more sensitive to the negative impact that their rhetoric can have on community perception and conduct. If the church were successful in getting politicians to see themselves as instruments of peace and unity, it would have significantly influenced the character the Jamaican politics.

Unity of Church and Community

There is growing awareness that there is a close relationship between the unity of the church and the unity of the human-community. In fact, the case can be made that the unity of communities and the overcoming of violence will not be achieved, if there isn't unity in the Christian community, which is present in every single corner of Jamaica. There are communities, both rural and urban, where the only stable and credible community leadership that exists, is that offered by the church. The Jamaica Council of Churches reiterated its awareness of this relationship recently, in its reflection on the piecemeal efforts to address the issues of crime and violence and other national problems. The AGM of the Council mandated the executive to approach the other umbrella groups of churches in Jamaica, to discern how partnership may deepen around questions, such as the overcoming of violence.

The emergence of a deeper partnership within the Christian community is likely to have a positive effect on national life. Being extremely concerned about community unity and how political leaders seek to foster it, the church is giving close scrutiny to how the emerging leaders treat this issue. Supporters of political parties have come to see the attention their community gets as being dependent on the political representative. The disregard for communities believed to be supporting a different party has fostered community rivalry, which has further mutated into gang rivalry that is now a permanent feature of communal violence.

Fostering community unity is no longer an option. There will be no peace in this country without community unity and the just sharing of the nation's resources. The churches feel that they must bring their house in order, so that they can speak with some moral force on this question of unity. As the leadership for the political parties intensifies, then those contending for office should know that the church is watching how they deal with the question of unity, both within their party and within the wider Jamaican community.

We are concerned that a poor example is being set in how differences between those contending for office are settled. I hope the leadership of the churches will be bold in its denunciation of the rhetoric and public conduct that undermine unity and peace. I hope church leaders will also be bold in encouraging their membership to vote for those persons who show evidence of being able to manage their own differences, and who seem committed to community unity and peace.

TEACHERS NEED INSPIRATION, SEPTEMBER 5, 2004

When the poor performance of students in the recent CXC examinations is put alongside the poor working conditions of teachers and the low levels of motivation among students and teachers, it must be difficult for schools to begin the new academic year with a bang. So the question that comes to mind is, who will provide the encouragement and motivation for students and teachers to press ahead, when we are fed with a diet of an education sector in a dismal state? What reason will teachers have to resume school with zeal and excitement when the impression is so often given that they have failed miserably?

Encouragement is not likely to come from the Breakfast Club because neither the Government nor the JTA is taking them seriously. The brilliant hosts and guests of this programme have become frustrated from their several attempts to highlight the real problems of the education sector. One wonders why they bother even to raise the issues related to education, which generally amount to telling the Ministry of Education, the teachers and the schools that they all have it wrong; that the energy, the programmatic emphases and the resources are being put in the wrong place. But then, the Breakfast Club is not about giving inspiration.

Ill-Trained Basic School Teachers

One wonders whether the motivation can come from Dr. Ralph Thompson, who seems focused on the weakness of teachers at the level of the basic school. If I heard him correctly, the fundamental problem is that ill-trained basic school teachers thwart children, who are then catapulted into the primary and secondary levels. He seems to be saying that we will not have better student output until we have solved this basic problem. How will teachers at the primary, secondary and tertiary levels be inspired or motivated by this preoccupation? I doubt whether inspiration is going to come from Senator Anthony Johnson, the Opposition Spokesman on Education. The Senator seems to see the problems in the education sector as being the consequence of the low resources the Government gives to education. Looking at Barbados and Jamaica, he mentions the 14 percent of the budget that Barbados puts towards education compared with the 9 per cent or 10 per cent that the Jamaican Government puts. However, since the Government prides itself in the PATH [Programme of Advancement Through Heath and Education] and cost-sharing programmes, alongside other interventions, the low resources argument rings hollow in the midst of a national debt that is 150 per cent of GDP. It is not to be expected, then, that any change in resource level is going to come soon. The assertion that more resources must be put into education is therefore not likely to provide teachers with zeal for their work on a September morning.

And will Wilmot Perkins be a source of motivation, encouragement or inspiration this September morning? Not likely! One must admit, though, that he has thrown out the challenge to the University of the West Indies, which is for him an intellectual ghetto. The surprising thing about Perkins' description of the university is that he uses the term intellectual and yet it is not a reference to Perkins himself. He is running out of able persons to engage him in a proper conversation. As for the other levels of education, their most obvious achievement, if one listens to Perkins, is that they graduate illiterate persons. Those who are inspired by Perkins' analysis of education, must also be prepared to delight themselves in the glories of their underachievement.

The inspiration that the teachers will draw on in the face of the presentation of a hopeless and dismal situation this September morning may come from the Ministry of Education. The Ministry was bold and sensitive in its decision to give up their claim to recover the monies, which teachers were said to have received in overpayment. The inspiration may also come from the support of parents who know that the task of education is one that is shared between the home and the school.

Inspiration and Encouragement

Inspiration and encouragement will come from the past students who, out of appreciation for what their school did for them, are not content to stand aside and look, or, worse yet, only to curse their alma mater. They mentor, support and inspire a new generation of students who now sit where they sat; whose lot may be worse than theirs; who live in a society which is under the threat of forces that are inimical to peace and human well-being. Above all, the inspiration will come from the love teachers have for students and their commitment to moulding character. Teachers are people who have a vision, a hope that they can make a difference to the society. Those who will return this September will not do so because their salary or the society's general appreciation of their work impresses them. They will return in the hope that their efforts, though feeble, will still make a difference. They will hope that this generation of children can be directed to a life of peace, prosperity and productivity. They will return, not because the talkers in the media inspire them but because they put more hope in their own actions than in strong, discouraging talk.

WHOSE VICTORY IS THIS?
FEBRUARY 6, 2005

I am appalled that the recent ruling by the United Kingdom-based Privy Council on the attempt of the Jamaican Government to establish the Caribbean Court of Justice, as the country's final appellate court, is being hailed as a victory for Jamaica. It seems that as a consequence of this ruling, Jamaica will have to go a different route than the simple majority of the Parliament, in seeking to establish the court in its appellate jurisdiction. Clearly, it is a victory for the Jamaica Labour Party (JLP), the Jamaican Bar Association, the Independent Council for Human Rights and the pressure group Jamaicans for Justice.

However, I do not regard a victory for these groups as necessarily a victory for Jamaica. These groups, with the exception of the JLP, are not peoples' organisations. They are elitist pressure groups, which seem more committed to controlling the elected people's representatives than anything else. They are not interested in the masses of the Jamaican people. The Jamaican people did not name them as their spokespersons. The JLP, for its part, is always looking for political mileage because they seem unable to convince the broad electorate that that party is still capable of providing adequate leadership for the Jamaican people.

Notion of Referendum

They hoped that by raising the referendum flag they would conjure up the failed West Indies Federation, in which that party gained political capital. They have always used the notion of referendum to frighten the People's National Party (PNP) and they in turn seem to believe that the Jamaican people are too foolish to make a distinction between the experiments of the 1960s and now. Only the Lord in heaven knows what got into the heads of the PNP leadership to have gone down this track in arguing that there is no need for a referendum before the court is established. The thing they fear the most may be the thing that will cost them the most.

But let's get back to this idea of victory for the Jamaican people. When the children of Israel left Egypt, according to the Bible (Numbers 14: 2 and 4), all the Israelites complained against Moses and Aaron saying, "Would that we had died in Egypt . . . So they said to one another, let us choose a captain and go back to Egypt." It seems to me that that is the kind of victory that has been won by the Privy Council's ruling. The victory is a victory for those who want to go backwards. It is a ruling in favour of retardation. It is a ruling against progress towards self-determination. It is a ruling that plays nicely into the hands of those who have no confidence in the people of the region to be fair and just.

It is a ruling that reinforces the notion that justice that is given by those who regarded (and may still regard) themselves as our masters is the best because they know how to be impartial and they know what is best for us. It is a ruling that smacks of the same paternalism that we have come to know from Britain. It is a ruling that people like Mutty Perkins will rejoice in because they seem to hold the view that the state has failed, that we have made no progress since 1962 and also that things were better for us as a people under the colonial governance of Britain. In their view, it is better that we go back.

Sadly, the ruling by the Privy Council has to be accepted because we still have that court as our final court of appeal. We would be fools to think, though, that because they have made this ruling that they are correct. Worse than that, it would be foolish of us to think that these law lords are free from bias and self-interest. In their interpretation of the constitution, they have found the case put forward by the pressure groups and the JLP to be more convincing. This has challenged the government to rethink its strategy and maybe even to rethink its personnel.

Testing Real Commitment

The ruling is also an opportunity to test the real commitment of the JLP and the other groups, whether they are truly interested in cutting the knot that has tied us to 'Mother country.' If the suggestion made by the former leader of the Opposition is anything to go by, I do not believe that anyone of the victorious groups is in favour of severing ties with the United Kingdom-based Privy Council. According to Mr. Seaga, the appellate jurisdiction of the CCJ should be established for ten years on a trial basis, during which time the Privy Council would remain the final court. However, one cannot see why one would bother to approach an intermediary court when it is not a final court. That idea is simply rubbish and is only a camouflage for a half-hearted commitment to a regional integration process.

The JLP and the pressure groups can go ahead and gloat over a ruling that delays the advance towards full self-determination. It is only a pity that the ruling came at a time when we are looking again at the contribution that people like Bob Marley have made to the mental emancipation of the Jamaican people. I hardly think that the Rastafarians and those who appreciate their anti-Babylon position will rejoice in this ruling of the Privy Council, unless off course I misunderstand what Marley meant when he sang "emancipate yourself from mental slavery, none but ourselves can free our mind."

A BLOW TO POLITICAL BIGOTRY, FEBRUARY 9, 2005

by Delroy Chuck, an attorney-at-law and Opposition Member of Parliament

The ruling of the Judicial Committee of the Privy Council (JCPC) on the three Caribbean Court of Justice (CCJ) acts was a mighty blow to political bigotry and to those who believe politics "run things." It was an affirmation of the rule of law. It was a fitting reminder that the law of the constitution is supreme, even if it is only the right procedure to follow in amending it. Barbara Gayle, The Gleaner's court reporter, must be commended. To the best of my knowledge Ms. Gayle is neither a trained lawyer nor a university graduate, but she clearly discerned how simple the issue was that the JCPC had to decide. "It really is a simple point of law," Ms. Gayle notes in her column in Sunday's Gleaner, "and if one even applies the common sense approach to it, one can see that the appellants were correct from the outset—that the CCJ which is to be Jamaica's final appellate court, must have permanence by being entrenched." She continued: "The nation's judges are the guardians of the law and. in particular, the Constitution, which is the supreme law of the land, and it is very disheartening when our judges miss such a fundamental point of law."

Thompson's Self-Inflicted Damaged

Across the page, on the other side of the Sunday Gleaner, we easily discern why our leaders have failed us. Rev. Dr. Livingstone Thompson is, no doubt, a man of integrity, of supreme intellect, head of the Moravian Church in Jamaica, but, sadly, did himself much damage in his column "Whose victory is this?" With due respect to Barbara Gayle, if she can see a simple issue of law to be decided, why can't Dr. Thompson, a man with training in religion and morality? With obvious disappointment, he laments: "It is a ruling in favour of retardation. It is a ruling against progress . . . It is a ruling that smacks of . . . paternalism . . . " and so on. No doubt, Dr. Thompson in berating the law lords would want them to ignore the rule of law and the clear meaning of the Constitution; and support political decolonisation and progress. It gets worse; the Prime Minister of St. Lucia, Dr. Kenny Anthony, is obviously upset that the JCPC could make such a 'flawed' ruling. "In my view," he is reported in the Sunday Observer as saying, "The judgement is flawed and smacks of legal bigotry." I am disappointed with my good friend and erstwhile University of the West Indies (UWI) colleague. When he and I were at UWI, I was teaching esoteric subjects like the law of trusts, contract, criminology and company law, while he was teaching constitutional law, where he must have fully examined Hinds v The Queen, which is the legal precedent that Dr. Lloyd Barnett and other attorneys relied on to predict and secure the ultimate ruling.

Very few people would remember that the presiding head of the Judicial Board in this case was Lord Bingham of Cornwall who some years ago complained of the Caribbean workload. His comments then gave the clear impression that he wanted the Caribbean to get its final court of appeal and relieve the law lords of the unnecessary burden. Yet, unthinking commentators would want us to believe that the JCPC sought to preserve their tenure and continue their colonial paternalism of adjudicating for Jamaica. One commentator in another Sunday paper abused the JCPC and commented: "By its clever reading of the mind of our Parliament, the Privy Council gave itself a stay of execution and lives to fight the good fight another day."

Application of the Law

Whose victory is this? To those who believe it is a victory for backwardness, for colonial governance and a blow to the progressive forces, I urge them to read the judgment carefully. The law lords were simply applying the law, respecting the procedure of the Constitution and, actually, merely adopted the submissions of Dr. Barnett, the foremost Jamaican constitutional lawyer. I do not feel elated; I feel a sense of sadness. If our government, with so many lawyers in Parliament, with so many attorneys at their beck and call, cannot surrender to constitutional authority, so evident to even the uninitiated, then what will stop them from using politics to override everything, again, including the rule of law? The decision of the law lords in the CCJ acts as a wake-up call to thinking Jamaicans, to the members of the media who want to perform their duty well, to the church leaders, and to anyone who has the interests of Jamaica, to think clearly and independently, and not to be overtaken in the dark corners of politics, partisanship, passion and bigotry.

RAS NOAH AND THE HAWK: MAKING FUN OF GOD, MAY 1, 2005

From a religious point of view, Patrick Brown, the managing director and lyricist for the recent production Ras Noah and the Hawk, should be commended for using the medium of theatre to stimulate thought about his revelation and wonder that, "we (the world) could be perilously close to the edge of the tolerance level of the 'creator.'" My comments about the production, especially since I am not in the main an art critic, should in no way take away from Brown's intention to raise consciousness and to help the society to climb back towards a high moral ground. At the same time, however, I hope that the comments will help Brown and other producers so see that, although they are doing an act for the theatre, and comedy at that, it is not beyond critique from a theological and ethical point of view. In fact, I would suggest to those who do productions that draw on religious symbols and notions to avail themselves of relevant religious advice before finalising their act.

I went to see the production mainly for two reasons. The first is that it has in it three of my favourite actors, Glen Campbell, who plays the part of the Rastafarian, Noah, Oliver Samuels, the Butcher and Dahliah Harris as the story teller, Cass Cass. The second reason is that the TV ad for the production is extremely funny. It is a well-chosen scene of Ras Noah calling the names of the animals (although one should say creatures, as the list includes two mosquitos) that he wanted for the ark. Ras Noah, being a Rastafarian who keeps distance from pigs, is really offended and shouted "Fire!" when his father (Butcha) calls for two pigs. The scene advertising the comedy leads one to expect more than one actually gets from seeing the whole production, as some scenes go from being funny to being silly. The production is meant to be loosely based on the Genesis story of Noah and the Ark, although the close connection with the Biblical story makes the connection a little more than loose.

The Caricature

The parts of the production, which for me were no reasons for laughter, were the scenes in which fun was being made of God. The discomfort I felt had nothing to do with the fact that the actor doing the part of God, David Ffrench, also played the part of the Spliff, whose name incidentally was true to form, as it seems he could not end the marijuana joint, a spliff, he was making. I was not uncomfortable either with the fact the looters sought to beat "God," as that was reminiscent of the beating and scouring of Jesus prior to his crucifixion. One reason for my discomfort was the fact that someone actually appeared and said, "I am God." Not even Jesus was so bold! In the past, producers were content to use allusions or just a voice to symbolise the presence of God. The effect of this was that the audience, as well as the actors, was able to engage the idea of God's presence without descending into disrespect. God no doubt has a good sense of humour but the idea of God is certainly not a joke and should not be put forward as being amenable to caricature.

Another moment of discomfort was the interaction between Brown's "God" and the other actors. The verbal abuse of the character, which according to the story was really meant to symbolise God, was ironic and appalling, not funny. If this is what is being offered as an alternative to being "preachy" the directors should think again. Patrick Brown and the artistic Director Trevor Nairne should consider whether the caricature, as a result of the level to which it descended, has not had the opposite effect of the honourable intention they have to raise consciousness about God.

Laughing at God

When actors make fun of politicians, as they love to do, it creates an opportunity for the audience not only to laugh at the joke but also, in a certain way, to laugh at the politicians. An even more sinister move in the production, then, is that the audience was invited to laugh at God, even though Brown may not have intended it. He is probably right in the implication that people make fun of the idea of God that they have. In fact, people like Mutabaruka want us to understand that the Christian idea of God is nothing but a laughable attempt by Europeans to mask their deceit and to keep Africa and people of the African diaspora in "babylonish" captivity. In any effort to show the relevance and higher value of the African religious world-view he caricatures anything called Christian, as if there is some pure African world-view, untainted by other civilisations. His caricature and denigration of the Christian and other faiths will not win him converts.

Persons like Brown, who make use of the theatre to put their message into the public sphere, cannot be naïve about religious symbols and religious symbolism. I hope that the Rastafarians who see this production will also offer a critique about the way in which their faith is caricatured. I am not sure that having the actor shouting out Jah ad lib appreciates the pious and deeply religious meaning of the expression Jah, which is a shortened form of Jehovah, and a way in which the Rastafarian use the expression in their worship. One does not have to be an adherent of a particular religious tradition in order to show respect for its notions and symbols. Furthermore, comedy is no safe haven in which to demean the value of a religious symbol or expression.

AND THERE SHALL BE RAIN!
APRIL 3, 2005

There shall be yet six weeks of drought and behold, the drought shall be very severe but after that there will be rain." Thus, spoke Minister of Water, Donald Buchanan recently, in commenting on the current spell of drought that we are experiencing. He went on to say that it would be costing the government some JA$5 million per week to respond to this water crisis. The assertion of the minister reminds us of the story in Genesis, in which Pharaoh dreamt about the seven fat cows and seven lean cows. In the dream, the seven lean cows ate the seven fat cows. It was a disturbing dream for the Pharaoh and that was how Joseph, who was able to I interpret dreams, came into the picture. Joseph said the dream meant that there would be seven years of plenty, which would be followed by seven years of extremely severe famine. Joseph's interpretation is the converse of Minister Buchanan's assertion for, in the case of the latter, he expects the period of drought to be followed by a period of rain. As we know, though, that period of rain is expected to be followed by another period of drought, and so on.

Searching for Water

The cyclical pattern in the rainfall is not new. It was the same when I was growing up in Newport, South Manchester, years ago. The periods of drought were equally severe. At one stage we had only one tank and so before long we had to get the buckets and kerosene tins to go in search of water. My father kept cows, and so we had to carry water on our heads for these poor creatures, which had no conscience about the amount of water they drank. We would have wished they knew how to share but once the cow put its head in the drum of water, the head would come up only when the cow had had enough water or when the water was finished. I can remember the times when we had to drag one cow from the drum so that another would get some of the limited commodity. The same was the situation in the use of water in the home. We were very excited when my father built an air tank, because we not only had running water but we also could use the shower that required less water than the bath. Conservation of water was not an option and planning to reduce the negative impact of the crisis was an ongoing affair—our lives depended on it.

In due time, my father built a second tank twice the size of the first, so our water troubles were somewhat alleviated during the lean months. For my siblings and I, happiness was to see both tanks filled to the brim. This is why I am amazed at the approach that the governments over the years have had to the situation with water. During the 1980s, I lived in the Springfield area of St. Elizabeth, which has a relatively high incidence of rainfall. It was always a distress to see the amount of water that would go to waste, as it rained every day during certain months of the year. It was like clockwork. The rains bothered no one because it would come about the same time each day and people simply planned their lives around it.

Wasting Water

However, all that water would simply go to ground. I would have imagined that all that was needed was a large reservoir in the hills, from which stored water could be piped to the plains of Santa Cruz, which does not have an equally high incidence of rainfall. What is even more shameful is the fact that communities like Ginger Hill, Claremont, Crawle and YS are having a water crisis when it rains so heavily in those areas. People have to travel all the way from Ginger Hill to YS, no less than 15 kilometres in search of water. It was in order to mitigate the desperate situation that the Moravian Church built a 40, 000 gallon tank in Springfield to store water from the months of plenty. Similar projects have also been completed at Lititz, in St Elizabeth, Newport, Maidstone and Mizpah, in Manchester, as well as Carmel in Westmoreland. However, when the months of drought come, 40,000 gallons do not last very long. The situation with the water supply in other regions, especially in St. Elizabeth and Manchester, is pretty much the same.

Planning for Water

The time has come for the government to make better use of the months of plenty. We need a 'Joseph' to manage this crisis! It is inexcusable that we should allow so much water to go to ground during the rainy months and then to go crying to God during the drought. It is nothing but an irresponsible use of the country's resources to use $30 million for six weeks in one year, as a haphazard response to the crisis, when that money would be sufficient to construct a facility that could last for many years storing water for several lean months. The Government and communities must act quickly to reforest the hills that have been damaged by fire so that the incidence of rainfall can be kept stable or be improved.

The Moravian service agency, Unitas of Jamaica, has taken this challenge seriously and with the help of the Environmental Foundation of Jamaica, will be doing reforestation in certain communities in Manchester. Beyond that, however, greater effort must be made to catch and store the water during the months of plenty. Like Pharaoh, I had a dream: In my dream, I saw several lean cows and several fat cows. Then I looked and noticed that the fat cows were devouring lean cows. Then one of the fat cows turned and was coming now to devour me. I started to run but I could not see properly because it was raining. Then I jumped out of my sleep. I wonder what this means?

DAWN RITCH AND THE EDUCATED CLASS, JULY 3, 2005

Dawn's Ritch broadside against Prime Minister PJ Patterson, the PNP and people with advanced degrees in last Sunday's Gleaner (June 26, 2005) was really a smokescreen. Like her counterpart on radio, Wilmot Perkins, her concealed intention is to undermine the credibility of persons who have pursued further education. Perkins does a similar thing. He attacks the University of the West Indies, for claiming to contribute to the development of intellectuals, while Ritch attacks the PNP for claiming to appeal to intellectuals. On the one hand, Perkins claims to be calling attention to the poor performance of UWI, notwithstanding its ventures and the measurable outcomes. On the other hand, Ritch claims to be calling attention to hypocrisy in the PNP for its desire to attract people who have pursued further education into its ranks. These attacks, however, are of the same kind. They are designed to undermine the credibility of institutions that emphasise the value of further education and of the individuals who claim to have pursued it. Both Ritch and Perkins know that their own intellectual prowess is not verified by calling attention to apparent weaknesses or failings of others.

Further Education Is Not a Laugh

One cannot gainsay the value of education and advanced training to the wellbeing of the economy, therefore there is really no need to caricature institutions that are committed to that outcome. Indeed, organisations and institutions should be encouraged in their ventures not laughed at. There are many countries that are reaping the sweet reward of giving unapologetic priority to further education. For example, over forty years ago the Republic of Ireland invested heavily in further education. They expanded access to third level education, thus creating a highly skilled labour force. Today, the world's leading pharmaceutical companies and all the world leaders in computer manufacturing are based in Ireland for both research and production. The economy is growing continuously, with an ever increasing demand for labour. In an attempt to improve the rate of literacy in the adult population, the government offers incentives to those returning to education. One consequence of this priority given to education is the movement towards a completely literate population, which is less costly to govern. For example, I was pleased to see that for the population census in Ireland, the heads of households were expected to fill out the forms and have them ready for collection. No one sat with householders to have them fill in answers to basic questions.

It would seem too that India, despite squalor and poverty in several regions, has also been able to focus on the creation of a highly skilled labour force, which is being sought after today. The point being made is that the knock-on effect of an educated population is extensive and of significant economic value. For this reason I was saddened by absence of reference to education and educational institutions in the speeches made overseas recently by the Prime Minister and his deputy. Prime Minister Patterson was addressing businesspeople in China about business opportunities in Jamaica, while Mrs. Simpson-Miller was addressing the Jamaican Disapora in New York, about her vision for Jamaica. However, neither of the two zeroed in on the role of education. Naturally, everything cannot be said in one speech but the absence of the reference to the role of education is, to my mind, telling. (Incidentally, Mr. Seaga, former Opposition Leader, seemed also to have missed the role of education and educational institutions in his recent attempt to characterise the next Jamaican brand.) One can only encourage the government to continuously discern the connection between national development and education and not to be bullied by no-holds-barred-loud-mouth journalists, whose real interest in further education is suspect.

UTECH's Involvement in Entrepreneurial Research

Despite what Ritch and her friends may think, further education and an educated population will always be critical in Jamaica's development. The recent mention of the involvement of the University of Technology (UTECH) in a worldwide study in entrepreneurial research is commendable. It is an example of the critical role that educational institutions play in fostering economic activity. The National Commercial Bank and Digicel are set to sponsor UTECH's involvement in the worldwide project, which is to involve several leading institutions around the world. In the Republic of Ireland, the link between industry and academic research has resulted in the patenting of products for commercial production on an ongoing basis. The discovery of new and unique products is no longer sufficient. Their commercial value needs to be demonstrated, which is the value of the link between the classroom, the laboratory and the plant. All third level institutions, even theological colleges, should seek the support of the private sector in making research, development and production central to the work that they do.

Ritch's Project

Ritch and Perkins are leading a cadre of persons who are fixed in their gaze on the worst aspects of the nation. They obviously serve some good but it is amazing that they never see performances or developments worthy of mention. One can only assume that they understand themselves as iconoclasts, with no interest at all in building up. Evidently their role is to tear down, to expose the blight and to show the hypocrisy. Let those who wish to build do so. That is not a "Ritchian" or a "Perkinian" project. Building is not their job. Since they believe they play a valuable role, given their persistent presence in the media, let us grant them that, even though it is hard to see their value beyond self-mutilation. Let us allow them to press on, in the hope that one-day those who are blind to their value will come to appreciate it.

INDEPENDENCE AND DEVELOPMENT, AUGUST 7, 2005

There is an ironic coincidence between the celebration of Independence and the lawsuit brought by residents of Portmore, concerning the leg of Highway 2000 that will pass through their community. The residents, in exercising their rights under our 'independent' constitution, took the Minister of Transport to court over the use of 'their' property and the lack of provision of an alternate route for them to get home. The Minister of Transport, in defence of the provisions of the law under our 'independent' constitution, argued that the residents had it all wrong. It is certainly an indication of the journey we have travelled, as an independent nation, that residents can feel empowered to take the Government to court.

For my part, I regret that the residents of Portmore lost their case, seeing they were the underdogs in the situation. Their principled objection was that there is no other reasonable, alternative route to the highway on which they will have to pay to travel to and from home. In the judgement of the court, the alternative route, the Mandela Highway, is reasonable, sufficient and fulfils the requirements of the law. Of course, the citizens do not seem to be sincerely objecting to the construction of the highway. Notwithstanding the allegation in their second suit, which claims that their property is being compulsorily taken, it seems their main concern is that they will have no option but to pay to travel on the highway to and from work.

It is not surprising that they lost the case, though, because it seems the residents were ill-advised about the strength of their position. It is clear that the laws regarding land use, roads and mineral deposits in Jamaica are not primarily designed to protect the interests of individual users or groups of individuals. These laws appear to be structured in such a way as to give the advantage to the state. The assumption underlying these pro-state laws is that government will act in the interest of the majority and should not be prevented from doing so. One would not be surprised, then, if judges unwittingly operate with this assumption in mind. If they do, it would not be their fault because the assumption is fixed in the framework in which the laws were drafted in the first place. Needless to say, there are many times when that assumption proves to be wrong.

Low Blows

Notwithstanding the hope that the court will not hear the case about the compulsory acquisition of property and although the Law Academy in a recent article has argued that the triumph is good for the government, the Minister of Transport should be careful about gloating about this victory. With the likelihood of an appeal pending also, Minister Pickersgill may want to delay his elation. It is always counter-productive when the government wins a case against citizens. The Peoples' National Party (PNP) representatives for the area are likely to feel the effects of this outcome in the next poll. In fact, it is nothing short of a public relations disaster that the case should have gone to court at all. It is indicative of the fact that sufficient care was not taken to include the citizens in the development of the plans along the way.

The Government has therefore benefited from two low blows. In the first place it failed to include the citizens in a manner that would take their concerns into consideration at the earliest point, so as to obviate the need for this court action. Secondly, it has won a case against an ill-informed group of citizens.

Haphazard Development

However, there is another issue about the motorway other than residents' concern about property, pay and alternate route. It has to do with the development policy being pursued by the Government, as they further the cause of independent Jamaica. In a July 15, 2005 press release, the Jamaica Information Service (JIS) reported that "the Ministry of Development is developing a comprehensive 20-year development plan to monitor the various socio-economic investments expected to emerge from the Portmore to Clarendon stretch of Highway 2000." The idea, according to the Minister Paul Robertson, is that the road would create space for development, where it now does not exist. He reiterated that the developments would not be allowed to take place in a haphazard fashion.

This issue of haphazard development is what concerns me because we do not know nor have we heard of the processes to guarantee proper development, neither have we heard of the plan for consultation with residents. As it ought to have been with the Toll Road, the developments being considered should be posted in a public place to be scrutinised by residents, especially those who will be directly affected. As it is today, only those directly involved in the construction of Highway 2000 seem to know the plan and its exact route. Even where the road will not pass close to any residential community, the route should be made a matter of public interest and scrutiny. Serious objections must be raised especially where sites of historical or environmental significance are to be affected.

Since the development of the Mona area, it seems that haphazard development has been the order of the day. The whole Portmore area is a case in point. Residents are allowed to do all kinds of additions to their property, without care being taken about how it affects the overall appearance of the area and the extent to which these additions impinge on the property of others. The lack of proper development is also evident in the buildings outside the University Hospital and along the garages along the May Pen bypass.

THE ETHICS OF FUNDING EDUCATION, SEPTEMBER 4, 2005

The wish of the government to annex some of the excess National Housing Trust (NHT) funds for use in education has become a major ethical issue. As I have heard it, the main objection is that the money was received as money for housing and should be kept as such (Edward Seaga et al). The Trust has not completed its mandate for providing houses for lower income persons and there is a continual expansion of squatter communities. It is by wishing to treat the trust as sacrosanct that Mr. Seaga has suggested that casino gambling should be used instead to fund the educational reform, since the proposed raiding of the NHT purse, in any case, cannot complete the job that needs to be done. Using the NHT funds for education will set a bad precedence, in terms of fiscal discipline. It is the thin edge of the wedge in fiddling with designated funds, which will provide the justification for dipping into other funds. The recent move to dip into National Insurance Scheme fund is a case in point.

New Resources

However, the decision to use the NHT funds must be seen as a judgement call. In the critical situation of the education sector, the Government has four options to access urgent additional resources: (1) create new resources (2) borrow (3) increase taxation (4) re-allocate current resources. The efforts to create new resources is an ongoing task, the outcome of which tends to be more medium-term and long-term than short term. For several reasons, the success of governments in this area has been at best mediocre or poor. Clearly, if we had a track record of creating wealth, the present discussion would not be taking place. Nevertheless, the Government may want to look seriously at this option because this is the only way to ensure a sustained response to the demand for money, which education, like other sectors will have in the coming years. While we await successful attempts at wealth creation, however, the needs in education stare us in the face. It is a luxury to pontificate about what could have been done to save us from this hour, without at the same time seeking to address the needs before us.

The second option is borrowing. I suspect there would not be any outcry if the Government had secured another loan from the World Bank for the same purpose. The point is that we have become so used to being in debt that we seem to regard indebtedness as an everlasting norm. As much as debt may be recurring, the salvation for Jamaica is not everlasting debt. Future governments must stake their credibility on the success of their efforts to release the nation from this debt stranglehold.

Taxation

To my mind, then, we should avoid increasing the nation's debt burden whenever we have an alternative, which means an argument in favour of borrowing for this cause cannot be accepted. The third option is taxation. I believe that unlike the case with borrowing, there would be a serious outcry at direct taxation—and rightly so! Increased taxation, without a reform of the tax policy, will only result in a greater burden for middle and lower income families. A way has to be found first to make the earners of higher income pay proportionately more tax, as they can absorb the greater burden.

Casino gambling, which is a form of indirect taxation, cannot be seen as a better ethical option either. The problem with gambling is the false hope of economic fortune it offers, while taking proportionately more from the poor. One should always keep in mind that while the rich may gamble for fun, for the poor it is no fun and games business. It is a serious attempt to get rich quickly. From an economical point of view, the benefits of gambling in general, or casino gambling in particular, are weighted heavily against the poor gambler. It would be a shame, then, to further prey upon the poor gambler while offering the hope of sweet success that 99 per cent of those who gamble will never see.

Reallocating Resources

The fourth option is the reallocation of resources. When considered alongside the other options, the Government's decision to go the route of reallocation of resources may be seen as fair ethical judgement. This conclusion is based on the fact that it has not been shown that the other options, as mentioned above, would result in a more desirable state of affairs. Moreover, the objections raised so far are not sufficient grounds for constructing a firewall around the excess funds. For example, the objection would be sustained if it were not the case that the Government is seeking a legal basis for their action. The objection would also be sustained if it were shown that other funds could be accessed with fewer negative consequences for the economy and more positive implications for good fiscal management.

The point, then, is this: when an ethical decision is made, those who challenge the decision must put forward arguments of a more convincing ethical quality. None of the arguments advanced so far are ethically superior to the choice to reallocate excess resources.

IS HANGING THE ANSWER TO CRIME?
NOVEMBER 6, 2005

Recently, a number of persons have been calling for the resumption of hanging. Given also comments made by the People's National Party (PNP) and the Jamaica Labour Party (JLP) spokespersons, it seems that it might be one of the issues on which the Government and Opposition will develop a common position. One gets the impression, though, that many of those persons calling for the resumption of hanging, as the main way of punishing persons convicted of murder, perceive the death penalty, as a silver bullet for crime, if one might excuse the analogy. If that is the perception I would advise caution. There are a number of reasons why someone advocating caution in the resumption of hanging will not easily be heard. Most people favour its reintroduction because there seems to be no other form of punishment that has equal capacity to deliver appeasement to the family and loved ones of those who have been murdered.

As the argument runs, those who have no respect for the lives of innocent victims should not enjoy the benefits of living. It is considered outrageous, if not unjust, for the resources of the state to be used to sustain the lives of those whose acts threaten or undermine the well-being of the state. Murderers have forfeited their right to life.

Strong Message of Community Intolerance

Another reason is that by putting murderers to death a strong message of community intolerance is sent to the perpetrators. Reticence on the part of recent governments to execute persons on death-row, who have exhausted their appeal process, has been considered by some as a sign of weakness or being soft on crime. It is further argued that criminals have been emboldened by this failure to press the law through to its bitter end. People feel that murders continue unabated not so much because the criminals are fearless but more so because they suspect that they will not be caught, tried and killed, if found guilty. It may well be that applying the death penalty will be a deterrent to persons contemplating murder. However, after witnessing how a mob killed and burned someone who attempted murder, and after hearing the family of murdered victims insisting that nothing short of the resurrection of their loved-ones will appease them, I no longer see capital punishment as an appropriate means of personal or communal appeasement. Apart from the likelihood of innocent persons being hanged, there is something about the death penalty that is irksome.

I am, therefore, not at a point of comfort with hanging, the firing squad, the electric chair or some lethal injection, as expressions of the value that I place on human life—even when the life in question is that a wretched murderer. In other words, the kinds of punishment we use are not only expressions of what we think about those convicted of heinous crimes but also expressions of the values of the community and what we think of ourselves. To say this is not in the least to be sympathetic to the merciless murderers, who do not think twice before erasing the lives of innocent victims. By saying that the death penalty is irksome to me I do not wish to trivialise the hurt and pain that relatives are feeling for the loss of their loved ones. It is evident though that people who are so lacking in mercy and feeling, so as to take someone else's life, are the products of the community and the society in which we live. There is something about the nature of our society that it throws up such wretched elements, with which reasonable people wish not to associate.

My fear is that by simply erasing the lives of the perpetrators we are exonerating the structures of the society that produce them. People must be held accountable for their actions but we would be very foolish to believe that what we are facing, in the spiralling murder rate, is simply individuals acting in a premeditated manner. There is a social system, a communal reality, in which murderers find succour and support. If the social system is predisposed to producing them then, like we saw in the movie, The Matrix, or as we see from the fiasco in Iraq, there is an endless stream of other potential murderers who will take their place. Something is added to our social milieu for each death that occurs and for how we respond to it and the way we treat the perpetrators when they are caught. The more hate and venom we pour into the social discourse (for example, blood for blood, fire for fire), the more of the same hate and venom the society produces. By adding blood to blood we should be surprised if the wanton wasting of lives become normal at the same rate we become desensitised to death and more death.

Changing the Discourse

The journey into this Jamaican abyss of murder and murderers did not come overnight. Therefore, neither the silver bullet of hanging, nor any improvement in our killing and life-erasing mechanisms is going to solve it. The time is right to change our discourse from one that honours life for some to one that honours life for all. My position, then, is that the heartless killers should not be allowed to determine our methodology of punishment nor to define the value and honour we place on human life.

EDUCATION OF PERSONS WITH DISABILITY, DECEMBER 4, 2005

With the International Day of Persons with Disabilities, December 3, coming so close to the World HIV/AIDS day, there is the possibility that the issue of disability will be overshadowed in our effort to digest the data relating to the AIDS pandemic. It is critical, though that we do not lose sight of issues that persons with disability are raising, which are not limited to the provision of wheelchair ramps, automatic doors and lifts.

Disability on the UN Agenda

In the wake of the increasing awareness of the human rights of all persons, the UN adopted, over thirty years ago, the Declaration of the Rights for mentally retarded persons. This was soon followed with the adoption of the Rights of Disabled Persons, in which the whole spectrum of human disability was highlighted. The aim of these declarations was to challenge the ill-treatment being experienced by such persons in several countries, Jamaica being no exception. Thirty to thirty-four years on there is still the need to raise awareness about the issue because persons with physical, mental, or other disabilities, continue to experience discrimination and hardships. Children in general have not yet learned that they must not mock and jeer their peer who is suffering from Downs Syndrome or cerebral palsy.

We have come a long way from the time when persons with disabilities would be hidden by their families to avoid stigmatising. The Government has recently signalled its intention to raise the profile of persons with disabilities by including them in appointments to its decision-making machinery and by the amendment of the Road Traffic Act to enable deaf persons to acquire a driving licence. These acts will certainly help to end the discrimination against disabled persons, which the UN declaration highlighted. The UN standardisation rules envisage two approaches to the education for persons with disability, which will depend on the financial ability and education tradition in the state. Some states have opted for the integrative approach, in which persons with disabilities are educated in mainstream schools. The School of Hope in St. Andrew is a good example of this mainstreaming approach. The alternative model is the provision of special schools, which is the model used in most countries. The Salvation Army School for the Blind and the schools for the deaf are good examples of the other approach.

Education Policy

The critical issues to assess, though, is whether the schools that respond to the special needs of persons with disability get the additional funding to respond to the greater costs for providing resources and equipment. The UN gave particular attention to this matter in the Standard Rules for an Equalisation of Opportunities for Persons with Disabilities, which the UN adopted in 1993. What was envisaged is that states would ensure, among other things, "that the public education programmes reflect in all their aspects, the principle of full participation and equality."

The Government may say that the vision enunciated in the report of the task force pays sufficient attention to persons with disability, as it clearly states the goal of education as including acquisition of social and life skills for all." Notwithstanding this laudable assertion, it is clear that the policy enunciated in the Education Task Force Report should be reviewed to take into consideration issues specifically affecting persons with disability. This would be a way in which we might indicate a mature awareness of the whole range of issues relating to disabilities.

The problem is that when one reads the report, the impression is formed that the Jamaican about whom the report speaks is presumed to be someone with all normal abilities. The failure to make special reference to persons with disability at critical points is a de facto exclusion of these persons because they are not, by and large, covered in general references. If one were to argue that the enunciated policy has in mind the needs of persons with disability, then one would need to show where in the task force report the issues are specifically mentioned. The report shows awareness of persons with physical disability mentioning the need for facilities for the physically challenged. However, the challenge to provide adequate access and support services, designed to meet the needs of persons with different abilities seemed not to have entered the equation at all. In chapter two, which deals with underachievement in education, where one would have expected to find the highlight of issues related to disability, the focus is on curriculum and behavioural issues. The implications for persons with disability are not even implied. One irony is that the section dealing with access to schools is concerned only with accessibility in terms of distance from school.

Great Need for Support Services

For persons with disability, there is a greater need for support services, whether in the form of individual assistance or with the provision of special equipment to facilitate learning. For example, when we speak of the use of computer technology, we should be mindful of the fact that needs are different for those who have full use of both hands from those who are unable to use their hands at all. Similarly a computer screen is of very little value to someone who is totally blind. The financial and social implications of these facts must be given visibility in a report of this kind.

THE DUPPY ECONOMIC POLICY, MAY 7, 2006

One of the challenges we face at this time each year, with the debate over the estimates for national expenditure, is to understand the direction the Government is taking, so that we can decide whether or not we want to journey with them. We also listen for the critique that the Opposition makes of the Government's economic policy, to help us understand the predicament in which we live. So far, however, we have seen more zeal than clarity and I do not feel closer to understanding the economic policy of either the Government or the Opposition. Minister of Finance, Mr. Audley Shaw, as is usually the case, waxed mightily on how to get the country to be indebted in a better way and Prime Minister Mr. Golding has lost me in a baffling array of weighty issues with no logical sequence. Together, Prime Minister and Finance Minister, give the impression that the average citizen is a spectator to his or her own destiny, over which they have been called to preside. At no point yet in the whole debate is it evident that individual electors can make a difference to the economy. For that reason it could be called a "Duppy" or "Ghost" policy because although we know it is present, we cannot discern it form or features.

Major Weakness

A major weakness in the present Budget Debate, then, is the absence of an economic vision in which the role of every citizen is understood. It is clear that the Government, or maybe more accurately the Finance Minister, does not wish (a) to return to a fixed exchange rate policy. That position, incidentally, is strongly supported by the directors of the International Monetary Fund (IMF). In the 2005 Article IV Consultation Report, which was published two days before the Budget Debate was opened, the IMF directors, "underscored the importance of maintaining a flexible exchange rate regime, aimed at safeguarding the external competitiveness of the economy." In addition to this policy, which the Finance Minister goes at unnecessary lengths to defend, it is also clear that the Government wishes to minimise waste in spending, control inflation and reduce the foreign debt. One has to say that these statements of intention express the vision of the Government but the Finance Minister has not said so. Now, if these points are central to the economic vision of the Government, in addition to listing them, there are some other things that it would be helpful for the Finance Minister to do.

Economic Policy Needs a Name

The first is that the minister could give the economic policy a name, that is, a simple description that even a secondary school child could understand. In order to understand the thing, we must know its name. If we do not know its name we will always be suspicious of it. In fact, one would have to say that because people do not know what the Finance Minister is talking about and how it relates to their decision making, they would be wise to have nothing to do with it. In the absence of a name, we shall then call this policy a 'Duppy Policy.' Knowing the name of the economic policy is part of what is involved with engaging with it. Jacob, [Genesis 32:24-28] wrestled all night with an angel [a duppy-like man] whose name he wanted to know and whose blessing he wanted to obtain, but we do not have all night.

Role of Private Citizens

The second thing that the Finance Minister needs to do with this 'Duppy Policy' is to indicate the role that he envisages for private citizens. I want to suggest that the most critical stakeholder in the economic and social life of the country is not the state, crucial though it is; it is not the Private Sector Organisation of Jamaica as important as that is; and it is not foreign direct investment as necessary as they may be. The Finance Minister was quite articulate about the role of the state, the private sector and foreign investment in facilitating growth. The way in which he seems to consider the private citizens is simply as recipients of social services, though, in my view, they are the most critical stake-holders. No doubt there is the need for so-called "hand-outs," not least because of the high unemployment rate, poverty and limited access to education and training. However, there are more progressive ways in which to connect private citizens to social policy than to use the old, tired terms of reducing unemployment and poverty, because in using them, citizens are only treated as statistical figures.

That older rhetoric should be replaced by the talk of facilitating empowerment. In this regard I must express my agreement with the Opposition Spokesman on Finance, who called for a clear policy on rural development. Mind you, there is also absent from the debate a clear policy on development in urban areas, which are trailing rural towns in desirable levels of living condition. The energy and rhetoric of Government should be focused on creating space for our creativity to be expressed and on removing the structures (both physical and mental) that inhibit the power of citizens. The Government, therefore, must be bold to name its economic policy and clearly enunciate the objectives, for in that way private citizens may both understand it and find a role in it for themselves.

IMPLICATIONS OF INDEPENDENCE, AUGUST 6, 2006

At midnight on August 5, 1962, the British flag was lowered and the Jamaican flag was hoisted for the first time, symbolising the birth of an independent Jamaica. The granting of Independence to Jamaica, if one can use that awkward expression, was another in a series of events to mark the break-up of the British Empire. At the height of its glory, the British Empire consisted of some 100 colonial territories. It is well established that local revolts and the declining viability of the sugar economy were the real issues behind the readiness to grant independence to places like Jamaica.

Beginning of the End

Although some British historians might not see it that way, the Declaration of Independence by Ireland in 1916 symbolised and set in motion the process of British territorial disintegration. According to the seven Irish nationals who signed the declaration on behalf of the Provisional Irish Government, "We hereby proclaim the Irish republic as a Sovereign Independent State, and we pledge our lives and the lives of our comrades-in-arms to the cause of its freedom, of its welfare, and of its exaltation among the nations."

There is, however, a difference between the Irish Declaration and the rest that were to follow, including that of Jamaica. Unlike others, the Irish did not wait to be granted independence, as if it were something to be granted, but declared their right to have it and took the initiative themselves to secure it by cutting the umbilical cord and to live with the consequences. There are still about 15 territories, including the Cayman Islands and the Turks and Caicos Islands, which see little to be gained from cutting the cord that ties them to Britain in a special way. Like Wilmot Perkins and others here in Jamaica, these tied territories say that, as a colonies, life is better and the future is more secure and that they are not prepared for the consequences of separation.

Mind you, the persistent economic captivity of former colonies like Jamaica makes the wish for restoration of those old ties understandable. Unfortunately for those voices, the processes of liberation and independence are irreversible. The yearning for independence among nations and peoples of the world is ongoing, as are the efforts to subjugate and control. The integrity of our own struggles, for emancipation and subsequent independence, requires that we in Jamaica aren't bullied by the threat of economic sanctions but come to the support of peoples' right for independence.

Jamaicans are inclined to zero-in on the economy when we talk about independence because we are not sufficiently clear on the national and international uses and misuses of political power that determine our economic fortune. In the Caribbean, the right to self-determination and the challenges for that struggle are probably best expressed in the Cuban experiment and the attitude of the U.S. to it. In the Middle East, the yearning for complete independence has recently escalated into a senseless, one-sided war, in which the U.S. seems to be siding with Israel in fighting a war against Iran by proxy.

However, whether we consider economic blockade, as in Cuba, or political subjugation, as in the current re-invasion of Lebanon, or poverty and violence, as in Jamaica, the consequences of the stifling of independence struggles and the failure to meet the aspirations for development and economic security lead to violence and instability. The connections between peace and the human struggle for development and self-determination were clearly expressed in the U.N. resolution on independence, which was adopted two years before Jamaica's independence, despite the abstention of Britain.

Independence, Security, Peace

The U.N. Resolution 1514 of December 14, 1960, noted that the continued existence of colonialism prevented the development of international economic cooperation and the ideal of universal peace. The resolution was forthright in its assertion that, "the subjection of peoples to alien subjugation, domination and exploitation constitutes a denial of fundamental human rights, is contrary to the Charter of the United Nations and is an impediment to the promotion of world peace and cooperation." The "hawks" in Israel and the American White House, the present British Prime Minister and my friend Ian Boyne are alike in their failure to see this link between independence, human rights, security and peace. They persist in the mistaken belief that the force of arms will be able to turn back the drive for full liberation that groups like Hamas and Hezbollah are seeking. If these groups were free, felt that their human rights were being respected and believed that their hope and economic fortunes were not under threat, they would have no basis for aggression.

Respecting Rights

The 1960 U.N. Resolution on independence further stated that "all armed action or repressive measures of all kinds directed against dependent peoples shall cease in order to enable them to exercise, peacefully and freely, their right to complete independence, and the integrity of their national territory shall be respected." People insisting that their rights be respected and that their complete independence not be stymied are given different descriptions today. Mr. Blair refers to them as the "arc of extremism," Mr. Bush calls them the "axis of evil" and Ian Boyne refers to them as religious fanatics. However, when compared to the slave revolts in Jamaica and the war for independence in America, these legitimate efforts for independence and respect differ only in the kinds of weapons, the means of warfare and the rhetoric.

NEW ELECTORAL COMMISSION: COSMETIC CHANGE ONLY?
DECEMBER 3, 2006

The recent swearing-in of the Electoral Commission represents, some have said, a significant forward movement in the structural development of the system of governance in our country. This development has been in the womb of the political system since the 1978 Representation of the People Interim Reform Act. A commission free from political interference was seen as a necessary safeguard for the credibility of the electoral process. With this development, the independence of electoral oversight, which evidently was in question, is now protected by the constitution. Given the outgoing Electoral Advisory Committee (EAC) chairman's recent sense of disgust with the delay in bringing about this action, he should be very pleased with the development.

I suppose we should be 'oohing' and 'aahing' about the change but I find that I am not as excited as one might have expected, and can't seem to put my finger on why this is so. It may be that I am simply unschooled in the finer art of electoral management. This is true, at least to some extent because I did not even see when a copy of the EAC recommendations and the relevant bill were made public. It could also be that my lukewarm response may be related to the fact that although the commission has a different status from the EAC and will report differently, there is not expected to be any difference in operations or deliverables arising from this change.

Like the Predecessor

When the Parliament approved the recommendations of the EAC and cleared the way for the change, the high-quality performance of the EAC was highlighted. Speaking in mid-2005, Dr Peter Phillips said that the work of the EAC is "one of the success stories of the country." If this were true, we might be guilty of having fixed something that was not broken. There are a number of reasons why the present Electoral Commission is not expected to outperform its predecessor in either the short or medium run. First, the internal structure of the commission will be more or less the same as what operated under the former EAC. The EAC had members who were there to represent the interests of their party, and there were other members, who were not expected to represent any party interest. As I understand it, the present commission has four nominated members, two each from the Prime Minister and the Leader of the Opposition. Additionally, there are four members who, although having a somewhat hazy nominations process, are appointed by the Governor General after consultation with the Prime Minister and Leader of the Opposition – exactly as it was in the previous dispensation. Some clarity about who might put forward the names of these other four members would be helpful. The ninth member of the commission will be the director of elections, who would have been recommended by the eight members already appointed. This manner of deciding on the director of elections is probably the only real difference in the internal structure. Even so, it is not expected to result in any real difference, as I imagine that the recommendation will likewise result from a transparent, interview process in which the best applicant for the position is chosen.

The second reason why we should not expect any immediate, improved performance from the commission is that there is as yet no change in the personalities for selected membership. Barring any radically new matter of ethics or morality, they are, therefore, expected to decide along the lines they have been deciding. Furthermore, with the former chairman of the now dissolved EAC selected to the commission, it is unlikely that the members are going to elect a different person as chairman of the commission. Finally, the director of elections under the EAC, Danville Walker, who has been doing a fine job, is continuing as director under the commission. So, considering the internal structure and the personalities, we should really see the commission as the same EAC in new clothes.

Opportunity Missed

Finding persons with unquestioned credibility and who enjoy the confidence of the political parties, takes care and thought. Happily, throughout the life of the EAC, the selectors have made good judgements about both members and directors of election. The difficulty the selectors must have faced with the naming of this commission, then, must have been how to exclude a person whose performance has been of a high quality. In fact, my fear is that with the same personalities and the same structures, the commission will carry forward the same thinking, the same fears, the same inertia and the same caution, which to my mind were the real humbugs they had operating as the EAC. It would be unrealistic, then, to think that the priorities of the same personalities, under the same chairman, with the same director of elections, will change simply with the change of status. I do not, therefore, think that we are any closer now to deciding on the issues relating to campaign financing—despite protests I hear to the contrary.

No Visible Difference

I am not privy to the argument that demonstrates what will be accomplished now under the commission that could not have been accomplished before under the EAC. So, I have concluded that the status of the EAC was more an issue for its members than for the rest of us, who are more concerned with deliverables. I suppose that in time, the real and visible difference of having a commission instead of a committee, apart from the question of status, will become clear. Otherwise, a change, without corresponding improvement in the quality of outcomes, would have to be called cosmetic.

CRIME AND DIVINE INTERVENTION, JANUARY 7, 2007

The 2006 rate of homicide in the Republic of Ireland may well see a 10 per cent increase over the figure for 2005. That is significantly different from the rate in Jamaica, which has seen a 20 per cent fall in murders in 2006. These are percentages though because, as shall see, the figures themselves tell a different story. The total deaths classified murder in Ireland in 2005 was put at 54. Additionally, there were four deaths classified as manslaughter, making a grand total of 58 homicides, which was 17 per cent over 2004. The situation deteriorated in 2006, with the total expected to fall somewhere around 64. If the official figures from the Garda (Police) Headquarters corroborate the figures we already have from the Garda Information Centre, there would be a 10 per cent increase in 2006 over 2005. An observer has remarked that this year could be the worst ever, in terms of murder rate, for the republic. From a statistical point of view, Jamaica has outperformed the Republic of Ireland in reducing homicide. This is the beauty of statistics.

When we hear that there has been a 20 per cent fall in murders, in Jamaica, we might be inclined to take more comfort than we should. Certainly that is the impression we get from those anxious to verify the credibility of Prophet Phillip Phinn. However, when we compare the 10 per cent increase in Ireland coming in the region of 64 and a 20 per cent decrease in Jamaica settling at 1,300, there is little reason for taking comfort. There is simply no justification for the rate of murder in Jamaica to be this high. If the Republic of Ireland is getting worried that they have passed 50 homicides in one year, then we should have no semblance of comfort until we have been able to reduce the total in Jamaica to a figure below 50 murders. It may seem impossible, but it calls for continuing disgust against the numbers, determination and a consistent application of those same strategies, which led to the 20 per cent reduction last year. The population of Ireland is nearly twice that of Jamaica and both countries have had a similar colonial and violent past.

Our communities are equally deserving of evidence that we respect human life.

Crime Prevention Programme

The reduction in crime is probably a direct result of the strategies which Commissioner Lucius Thomas outlined a year ago. Serious attempts have been made to improve the divisional intelligence units and the use of forensic science. The Major Investigation Task Force (MIT) was set up to target specific geographical areas known for their high murder rates. We hope that the work of that task force will be evaluated to secure improvement and that more resources will be provided for its work. We must also encourage the Minister of National Security to press ahead with the plans he announced in May for the establishment of a crime prevention programme for each parish. The overall programme, which was detailed in the sectoral debate by Derrick Kellier, involves building the capacity of communities to prevent crime and enhancing the capabilities of the police to detect and counter criminal activity. Evidently, the MIT is located within this broader policy and has already begun to justify its establishment.

Those of us who pray for divine intervention into our crime problem should be mindful of these crime-prevention measures when we pray. In fact, these programmes should be the focus of our attention rather than the prophecies about crime reduction. We are fooling ourselves about how the Lord will intervene, consequent on our prayer and fasting, if we fail to implement programmes with those aims and objectives, as the Hon. Derrick Kellier outlined, and which have been mentioned again and again in the different task forces on violence and crime.

No Time for Despair

The protracted problems with serious crime coupled with failed policies of crime reduction can cause people to despair. It is for this reason people have become fascinated by prophecies about what the future holds for crime. It is for the same reason people are drawn to horoscopes. Despair evidences itself in our wanting to see the future, which, if positive, lulls us into a false sense of security. Looking for prophecies about the future can be a substitute for hard work and initiative and is constructed on the erroneous belief that someone is going to work the problem out for us.

Colin Steer, writing in last Tuesday's Gleaner, admonished us not to be preoccupied with the shallowness that may parade as prophecy. This is a timely admonition. Hanging on to the words of prophecy may indeed be shallowness. More than that, however, it is, as Jesus warned (John 12:39), the temptation into which an evil generation falls. Those of us praying for divine intervention and those of us seeking consolation in prophecies, should also be informed about the strategies that have worked to reduce murders in 2006 and link own our community efforts to them. Indeed, if the work of the police confirms the prophecies and the divine intervention that we seek takes the form of the effective strategies that led to the 20 per cent murder reduction in 2006, then let us prophesy and seek more of the same. Maybe Ireland could learn from what we are doing.

Chapter Two

Regional and International Issues

RELIGION ON THE CARIBBEAN AGENDA, JULY 6, 2003

The issue of religion was never expected to be an agenda item at a regional Heads of Government meeting. In the thinking of many, religious ideas and religious affiliation are not sufficiently important to detain the serious business of the region's leaders. Notwithstanding, it is not hard to show, taking the Caribbean region as a whole, that religions and religious affiliation are issues of social and economic significance.

Of the approximately 40 million people who live in this region, about 78 per cent (a little over 31 million) regard themselves as Christians, even though this figure does not coincide with the actual membership of the churches. In the case of Jamaica, of the 2.3 million people, about two million regard themselves as belonging to the Christian faith. About half that number, one million is listed as members of churches. Seven per cent of the Caribbean population belongs to what the authors of the World Christian Encyclopaedia refer to as Spiritists, being adherents of Afro-Caribbean, Asian and American religions that cannot be incorporated into the traditional designations. Examples of these would be the adherents of Voodoo in Haiti, the Bedwardites and Rastafarians in Jamaica and the Jordanites in Guyana. Hindus account for two per cent of the region's population, Muslims one per cent and Jews, Bahais, Buddhists and some new religions account for another one per cent. 11% of people in the Caribbean regard themselves as having no religious affiliation. Of course, the fact that 89% of people in the region claim a religious affiliation may be of no more significance than if 89% went bed after 9:00 p.m. or if 89% prefer coffee to tea. In other words, we treat the issue of religions and religious affiliation as a matter of personal choice that need not have any social nor economic significance.

And yet, if 89% the region's population is in bed at 9:00 p.m., that will have implications for advertising and television programming. Furthermore, one does not have to stretch one's imagination too far to see the economic implications of 89% of region's population having a preference for coffee. We must then re-think this idea that because religion is a matter of personal choice it does not merit serious scrutiny and analysis to come to terms with its economic and social import.

Admittedly, one of the problems with religions and religious affiliation is the degree of diversity. If we take Jamaica, for example, the million members of the Christian faith are spread among no less than 60 major denominations with numbers between 150,000 and 200 members and a mindboggling number of other independent bodies. However, the plurality of churches is not much different from the plurality of companies that are registered. We have as much data about one as we have about the other. Therefore, while we sympathise with those who confess being unable to keep up with the nuances or the differences between the religious groups, we cannot have the same sympathy for those who would want to dismiss them because they do not have the time to do the research to understand them.

Social Issues

The problem of religious plurality aside, there is no need to try to justify the social significance of religion in the society. Emile Durkheim, one of the fathers of modern sociology, argued long ago that if religion has given birth to all that is essential to society, it is because the idea of society is the soul of religion (The Elementary Forms of Religious Life, 1912). It is long recognised that the symbols that are systemised into a religious group have both psychological and political effects and relate to the perception of problems and solutions in the society. A group like Jamaica's Fellowship Tabernacle is a good case in point. The charismatic leader of the church, like others before him, could not resist the urge to enter the political fray because he believed he was under a divine command so to do. The idea of the will of the Lord expresses itself in political ambitions.

From a sociological point of view, it is also important to observe how theological language is used to describe what can also be called psychological or psycho-social issues. For example, where the older Protestant and Roman Catholic churches speak say of homosexuality as a sinful orientation, the charismatics refer to it as an evidence of demon possession. To the charismatics, it is not just a sin that God will forgive; it is caused by a demon that must be exorcised through the power of the Holy Spirit and the instrumentality of the authority of the religious leader. Unless we can appreciate the symbolic world in which 89% of the region's population operate, we can neither claim that we understand the population nor will we be able to bring about the kind of regional transformation that we desire. It may be, then, that religion, religious affiliation and religious ideas are more critical to regional solutions than we think.

CARICOM, THE UN AND MORAL/ETHICAL PRINCIPLES, MARCH 7, 2004

The apparent political naivety of the Caribbean Community, (CARICOM) and the Patterson administration in seeking the involvement of the UN Peace Keeping Force in Haiti, without the clear indication of the support of the USA, is breath-taking. One gets the impression that Minister Knight, acting for CARICOM, approached his task intent on making a case for the involvement of the UN Security Council on the basis of some high moral or ethical position. According to Mr. Knight in his presentation to the Security Council, CARICOM's position was not motivated by the desire to promote the political interests of any particular personality in Haiti, but "was based on the need to remain faithful to democratic principle [s] and the integrity of constitutional order."

The irony is that the very day the Council rejected the request for a peacekeeping force in Haiti it sanctioned a peacekeeping force for Cote d'Ivoire. In his report to the Security Council, the Secretary General himself expressed the same concern in the same language as Minister Knight. According to the report on Cote d'Ivoire, "the prolonged political stalemate could have taken a turn for the worse with recent attempt by the Young Patriots to break the cease-fire. In language akin to the Secretary General, Mr. Knight said, "the situation [in Haiti] had now reached crisis proportions, given the continuing breakdown in law and order." In its resolution concerning Cote d'Ivoire the UN declared that it is committed to, "the sovereignty, independence, territorial integrity and unity of Cote d'Ivoire," and that by the resolution it was calling attention to, "the importance of the principles of good neighbourliness, non-interference and regional co-operation." These are the very principles that the CARICOM would wish to uphold for Haiti so, what is the difference?

What CARICOM missed is that the Security Council is not swayed so much by ethical and moral principles as it is by sheer political pragmatism. The recent involvement or non-involvement in Iraq is only one of several cases in point. The UN Security Council is under the de facto administration of the USA primarily. To have sought the involvement of the Security Council without assurance of the support of the USA is either sheer naivety or insincerity. Mr. Knight was at pains, with Prime Minister Patterson, to say they are concerned with democratic principles and the rule of law. In truth and in fact, the net effect of that concern was the propping up of Mr. Aristide. The subsequent abduction of Mr Aristide shows that the USA was not concerned with securing a role for him in the solution to the crisis, which means the UN Security Council could not have supported CARICOM's position. The rule of thumb, which the regional leaders should have known, is that the UN Security Council will only support resolutions that the USA sponsors or support. The regional leaders should have known the position of the USA on the matter before exposing themselves to ridicule by having their resolution defeated and a mockery made of their position by the casting aside of Mr. Aristide.

The Credibility of the UN

Many persons are now of the view that the way the UN Secretary General, and the UN community in general, responded to the Iraq crisis, has seriously undermined and eroded the credibility of the UN. That body, then, should not be expected in this dispensation to rise to the heights of moral and ethical rectitude. We live in an unreal world if we imagine that the UN operates with impartiality and neutrality. By attempting to perpetuate these false notions the UN peacekeeping forces have overseen disasters in Somalia (1993), Rwanda (1994), and Bosnia (1992-95), where they refused take the sides of the victims. It is evident that the UN force could take the sides of victims, when they were under the tutelage of USA foreign policy? CARICOM must wake up and realise that the UN is no longer, if ever, a superior moral authority to national governments. It responds to the interests of the member nations, with the interest of the most powerful in military and economic terms, of both, having the day. To deal via the UN Security Council's involvement in the region means getting into bed with the USA.

A Blessing in Disguise

The non-involvement of the UN in Haiti, though, is probably a blessing in disguise. The likely outcome of that involvement would be that CARICOM member states would be obliged to send their troops to serve for the UN and to further the interest of the USA. The fact that the USA has chosen to enter Haiti on its own, which is only a smaller version of the entry into Iraq, gives CARICOM the option not to be a part of that military initiative. Although it must be said that our need for USA funds may mean we cannot refuse the invitation of the USA to help to give retroactive credibility to the abduction of Aristide. The move is hewn out of the same principles that led to the Iraq invasion and the subsequent complicity of states that opposed in the first instance. Now, we no longer are allowed to raise questions of the credibility of the move in the first place.

What I hope CARICOM will do is refuse to be part of the USA Haiti initiative. However, that refusal to participate should not be articulated in some moral or ethical code. It should be refused on the ground of financial inability because that language of money will make more sense to the USA than talk about democratic principles and high notions of morality and ethics. If we need a world body that will act consistently in defence of moral and ethical principles, we have to look elsewhere because with its present rules of engagement and political interests the UN cannot perform that role.

A CRISIS IN HUMAN SEXUALITY, DECEMBER 5, 2004

Current discussions in the society about homosexuality, heterosexuality and the spread of HIV/AIDS have revealed that we are seeing in our time a crisis in human sexuality and sexual practices. In Jamaica, as indeed in other societies, we know that we are facing a crisis when there is a strong call for the church, by which is meant the leaders representing the Christian community, to speak out. It is reasonable to expect that representatives of the largest religious community should speak at a time as this because the issues related to the crisis touch on the lives of members of that community. It is also true that when, in the Christian community, we make reference to the will of God for human lives and when we implore people to try to discern what that will is, it is often frowned upon as empty rhetoric. However, the way we respond to the perceived crisis in human sexuality and sexual practices will depend principally on how we understand the human being, that is, on our anthropology.

Cultural Preference

There are two trends in sexuality that when seen together create the sense of crisis. One is the impression we have that a traditional Jamaican cultural preference of recognising heterosexual relations as the only legitimate form of sexual relations, is under political and economic pressure to adjust to the cultural preferences of North America and Europe, both of which have different understandings of legitimate sexual relations. The traditional Christian understanding of the human being influences the Jamaican position, which shows a preference for heterosexual relations. In other words then, the practice of homosexuality is a cultural preference constructed on a certain notion of the human being and the arguments that try to justify the practice otherwise have not been convincing.

The other trend that has helped to create a sense of crisis is the statistics about HIV/AIDS which was released in observation World AIDS Day, December 1. The trend in the data is troubling, as it reveals a rapid rate of infection in Jamaica which, like other developing countries, seems to have the conditions that favour the spread of the disease. We were led by both national and international presentation of the data to focus on the impact that HIV/AIDS is having on the lives of women, as the faster rate of infection among them reveals that they are more at risk of infection than men. At the same time, however, it is well known that the disease is spreading mostly through heterosexual contacts. I believe then that to have focused mainly on the impact on women, rather than on male sexual behaviour, was misguided. If the rate is increasing more amongst women, in a society where men have several sexual partners, the conclusion must be that male sexual conduct is most responsible for the spread. There is clearly a gender imbalance in the research and analysis of the data. We seem to need a more gender sensitive presentation of the data on HIV/AIDS that hold conducts and impact in tension.

The problems of human sexuality, which are expressed in the issues relating to homosexuality, heterosexuality and HIV/AIDS, stem principally from how we understand the human being, i.e. anthropology. Let's consider first practices of homosexuality and heterosexuality: In the view of many, it does not matter what people do in the privacy of their homes, providing it does not prejudice the rights of others and the public interest. Therefore, the argument continues, the sexual relations that are practised between two consenting adults in the privacy of their homes really should trouble no one and should not be the subject of legislation. The same argument is used to justify the smoking of marijuana. Happily, it has not yet been used to justify bestiality. The limits of that argument are illustrated by the call on one hand to decriminalise sodomy in the privacy of the home and, on the other hand, a call to make a person with HIV/AIDS having unprotected sex to be guilty of a criminal offence. We cannot have it both ways.

The argument about privacy and consenting adults is really an argument about the freedom of the individual, which is always to be mentioned in any definition of the human being. The centrality of freedom to the understanding of the human being is illustrated by the number of times it appears in the Charter of Rights and Freedom in our Constitution: freedom of conscience, freedom of expression, freedom of peaceful association, freedom of movement, freedom from discrimination. The question we seemed to have forgotten to ask, though, is where did this idea, that freedom belongs centrally to who the human being come from.

Choice and Responsible Action

The idea of the human being as a creature with freedom, free will and the capacity for choice is given to us from the Judeo-Christian tradition, which asserts that God created the human being in God's own image. Theories about how the world came into being, which have no reference to God as Creator, cannot account for this notion of freewill in the individual. It is a fallacy then, to speak about free will and the capacity for choice without appreciating that these ideas were first formulated in a theological framework that affirms a Creator who gives gifts to creatures. And if we speak of the free will of the individual, we must also speak about the will of the Creator. An anthropology that is centred on the freedom of the individual is a part of the Judeo-Christian heritage. However, that tradition is also one that emphasises responsibility to the community. In the Judeo-Christian account of creation, the importance of the wider community is emphasised in the creation of male and female in the image of God. In the Judeo-Christian tradition, authentic community life is therefore a life between the two separate sexes.

When we are faced with the confusion about homosexuality, the dangers of irresponsible heterosexual conduct and the threat of HIV/AIDS, the Christian community makes a plea for responsible human action in private for the well-being of the community. For this reason, an emphasis on the individual and individual rights that does not at the same time speak of the responsibility of the individual to promote the well-being of the community is a deficient anthropology. The point is that the sum total of all consulting adults, in homosexual or heterosexual relations in the privacy of their homes is what makes the community and has created for us a sense of crisis. Therefore, private conduct is also the business of the community because it should not be imagined that private conduct will have no direct or indirect community impact.

THE DEATH OF THOUSANDS: A THEOLOGICAL PROBLEM, JANUARY 1, 2005

The disaster visited upon the developing countries around the Indian Ocean seems to be a senseless destruction of lives and livelihood. The World Health Organisation (WHO) estimates that the death toll arising from the December 26, 2004 tsunami to be above 120,000. In Indonesia alone over 45,000 persons are confirmed dead in Sri Lanka well over 22, 000, and in India 7, 000. The scenes of people struggling to stay alive in the surging waters were horrific but more horrific were the scenes of the dead, many of them children, being buried in mass graves. It is believed that at some stages the waves were travelling up to 500 miles per hour. There was little warning and within three hours of the quake the damage was done at distances of over 1000 miles from the epicentre. One cannot begin to imagine the dislocation to the lives of the survivors, the threat of diseases and the lack of food and drinking water. Even with the frequent hurricanes and the occasional earth quake, the Caribbean knows nothing of the scale of this disaster and so the figure is simply mind-boggling. Recent seismic activity in our region, however, is warning enough that it could be literally wiped out by a natural disaster of this magnitude.

The scale of this disaster is probably the worst in recent memory. The grief is untold. Life on earth is so vulnerable in the face of such force. It seems to be senseless and purposeless; destruction with a cause but without reason. We seem unable to avoid the conclusion that the destruction is evidence of the anger and violence that is inherent in nature. A moment like this is probably easiest for the agnostic or the person who does not believe in an Almighty God. For them the disaster is an act of nature. It is a tragedy. No being, no God, no angel, no power in the heavens or on the earth has either caused it or could have prevented it. No blame is to be cast. No power except the power of nature is involved. The whole thing is simply regrettable. By the movements of the plates below the earth's surface a tsunami was created and it washed away everything in its path.

Where Is God?

To the person, especially from the Judeo Christian or Islamic tradition, who believes in the almighty loving God, the one who creates maintains and rules over the processes of nature, the destruction caused by the tsunami is a huge problem. That person is inclined to ask, "Where is God is all of this"? If God has control over the processes of nature and history, as the Bible affirms, then God must answer to the need for so many lives to be lost – thousands of children of the poor. Similarly, when Christians and Jews reflect on the centuries of the slave trade, the potato famine in Ireland, the genocide in Germany, Austria, Rwanda and Somalia, they also ask the question, where was God?

The tsunami came ashore at Christmas, when Christians were observing the feast of the incarnation, Immanuel, God with us. The doctrine of the incarnation may be explained as God in Jesus participating and sharing in all the realities of human life and history. In responding to the question of where God is in the disaster, some Christians say that God is not a passive observer but shares the grief of every grieving family.

The Hindu Tradition

God weeps with every child who is orphaned, with every person who has lost a spouse or children. The thing that these Christians find appealing is not

God's might to prevent death and destruction but God's love to over expose himself to human life. God is a suffering God and as the Easter feast affirms, God dies and rises again. Death is not the last word. The greater tendency in the Judeo-Christian and Islamic religious streams to centre the focus on the human being means there is great difficulty in these monotheistic faiths to answer the difficult question of the role of God in natural disasters. However, given the region of the world in which this disaster occurred we should look to the oldest theological tradition in that region to get a grasp of the theological problem that it may represent. A central theme in Hindu theology is that the whole universe is in a continuous process of destruction, dynamism and change, which is expressed in their teaching about reincarnation, rebirth and death. The events of the world happen in a cyclical fashion that repeats itself. There is no beginning or end for new beginnings follow every moment of destruction. So the cosmic process, like the annual cycle of the weather is marked by a succession of asymmetric cycles. Occasionally, the God Vishnu embodies part of himself in the world interrupting the cyclical processes in order to slow down the advance to disaster, since the destruction of this order is a surety. In Hindu theology, the God Vishnu has intervened 9 times in the present 3,893,086 years that have passed since this cycle of the present world. The inclination to destruction, therefore, inheres in the very character of the earth.

The Proper Question

The end of the present cycle is to be expected but it will be succeeded by another cycle—another world. The quake in the Indian Ocean is indicative of the ultimate deterioration and destruction of this present order. The tsunami has created health, economic and social problems, to which the energies and resources of the world must be organised to address. It seems, then, that failure to respond to the disaster and the misuse of the world resources in wars etc., is what constitutes the theological problem—not the tsunami itself. It may be that to ask where God is in the disaster is the wrong question. The question each person must ask is "How can I respond?"

THE CHURCH AND HUMAN SEXUALITY, MARCH 6, 2005

The subject of human sexuality is as controversial as it is complex. According to James Nelson (Embodiment: An Approach to Sexuality and Christian Theology, 1978) sexuality is our self-understanding and way of being in the world. It is who we are, we who experience the cognitive, physical and spiritual need for intimate communion. In his view, it includes three levels of experiences (a) masculine and feminine characteristic that are culturally determined, (b) intentional orientation towards others and (e) human relationships Phyllis Tremble in her book, God and the Rhetoric of Sexuality, 1978, sees sexuality in terms of human identity. Speaking with reference to the creation story in Genesis she said that the word for woman (isha) is not the meaning of a female but rather the recognition of sexuality. The creation of the woman is indicative of the sexual differentiation. For her, then, sexuality is about recognising that the human community is comprised of ish (man) and isha (woman).

Definition

I like the definition given by Philip Sherrard in Christianity and Eros: Essays on the Theme of Sexual Love, 2002. According to Sherrard, man really begins to experience his reality when he becomes aware of his sexual nature. Sexuality is not merely an accident of that reality. On the contrary it is the living, flowing energy whose physical aspect is but one mode of its expression. Human sexuality is the medium that puts him in contact with other realities and other incarnate selves. Our sexuality then, is not simply biology or psychology. It is the way we relate to the world as male and female beings. It is about our attitude towards our bodies and those of others.

The classical period in Church history is dominated by the figure of Augustine of Hippo (c.400). His writings on marriage and hence his view on human sexuality has set the overall pattern for thinking about these matters and has continued to the present day. In one of his better known works, Confessions, he details his emotional state as a sinner: "My one delight was to love and be loved. But in this I did not keep the measure of mind to mind which is the luminous line of friendship but from the muddy concupiscence of the flesh and the hot imagination of puberty mists steamed up to becloud and darken my heart so that I could not distinguish the white light of love from fog of lusts."

Cauldron of Illicit

Augustine said further that when he went came to Carthage he was caught up in a cauldron of illicit love. He was not yet in love but I was in love with love. He sought some object to love since he was in love with loving. The end result of Augustine's discourse was to reinforce the idea that the body is the source of sin and must be resisted. In general, the early Church Fathers had very negative things to say about the sexual body. Their attitude to sexual desire served to construe sexuality as something wrong and the woman's body as a threat. According to Jerome, marriage and wedlock should be praised only because they beget celibates. The analogy was that one gathers roses from thorns, gold from the earth; pearls from shells.

Sexuality in the early church was seen as a consequence of the Fall that went side-by-side with the loss of immortality. A typical interpretation of the Fall was that it was a fall from innocence into awareness of sexuality. From henceforth, it became difficult to dislodge the association between sin and the sexual act. Women were perceived as the harbingers of evil and sin. Occasionally, it was felt that the act of sexual intercourse itself was the means whereby original sin was transmitted from one generation to the next.

The Middle Ages

Attitudes in the Middle Ages did not change significantly but theologians were obliged by the authority of scripture to accept that procreation is a good end even though the act of sexual intercourse itself was not favourably described. It was in this period then that the insistence on marriage for the purpose of procreation took on the status of dogma. According to Roman Catholic teaching sexual intercourse for any other purpose than procreation was venial (or pardonable) sin for the married person but mortal sin for the unmarried. The dilemma for the church in the Middle Ages was that it had to agree that the coming together of man and woman in coition was a mystery related to the union of Christ and the Church, while at the same time insisting that the act ought to be only for bringing forth children. This insistence that procreation was the sole reason for sexual intercourse soon began to crumble under its own weight.

The attitude to sexuality in this period may be derived from how God was perceived. There was a shift from seeing God as immanent (present in all things) to seeing God as aloof. As it was agreed, God did not need human beings to do what He needed to be done in the world. The human body was not necessary for divine activity. There was no theological support for a dualism between mind and body. One of the off-shoots of this dualism was the subordination of women. Men abrogated to themselves the higher part of the dualism and projected upon women the lower half. Misogyny became rife in the Reformation period with the burning of witches. It is in the post-reformation period that the attitude to sexuality, as we know it today, was born.

LONG LIVE THE IRA, OCTOBER 2, 2005

Sinn Fein's rally in Dublin (Ireland) on Saturday, September 24, 2005, was another example of the party's smart political manoeuvring, but only in retrospect can the genius of the march be seen. Sinn Fein/IRA caused traffic jam and created a storm of protest by a march involving hundreds of children in what they called the centenary of the founding of the party. The Irish

Justice Minister and the Irish Independent newspaper tried to deny Sinn Fein's claim to the anniversary, but the party's media presence was bolstered two days later when the Irish Prime Minister, Taoiseach Bertie Ahern, declared (Monday 26/09/05) that "the IRA guns are gone." So, the IRA may be no more, but long live the IRA. The "guns are gone" declaration was made as Mr. Ahern responded to the report of the Independent International Commission (IIC), which was named to monitor the decommissioning of the weaponry of the paramilitary organisations. In a news conference in Northern Ireland earlier the same day, chairman of the commission, General de Chastelain and the two independent monitors, reported that to their certain knowledge, the whole arsenal of the IRA had been put beyond use.

For over 30 years the Irish Republican Army (IRA), which is in fact the military outfit of the Gerry Adams-led Sinn Fein, declared war on the British Government and sought to use force to drive them off the island. As the book Lost Lives revealed, a little over 3,000 persons were killed in the thirty-year conflict. Probably the worst atrocity was the 1998 Omagh bombing, in which 27 people were killed. The reason the IRA came into being was to continue the struggle for the full independence of Ireland from Britain.

Although the Republic won its independence in 1922, the Northern six counties are still under British rule. From the report, it seemed that the IIC had painstakingly watched as weapons, including mortars, machine guns, explosives, rockets and launchers were disabled. One suspects that they have been buried under concrete at some secret location on the island. In its efforts to build trust between itself and the paramilitary groups, the IIC accepted that the decommissioning of arms had to be conducted outside of the glare of the media. In any case, it seems only in this way would the IRA follow through on its commitment to decommission its arms. The IRA did not want their sincere attempt to move to a non-violent level of political involvement to appear as defeat. Journalists tried but in vain to get details of the actual amount of weapons that have been put beyond use. All they were told was that the amount was consistent with the listing made by the British and Irish security forces.

Time, Patience, and Investment

The roots of the violent conflict in Northern Ireland are different from the root causes of the violence we are experiencing in Jamaica. For that and other cultural and economic reasons, one cannot simply apply approaches used in Europe to inner-city Jamaica. However, despite the differences, there are at least two lessons that those at the forefront of efforts to bring lasting peace to Jamaican inner-city communities can learn. The first lesson is that ending violence takes a whole generation and lasting peace may take a whole lifetime. The report of the complete IRA decommissioning has come seven years after the Good-Friday Agreement, in which total disarmament of all paramilitary organisations was accepted by all parties, as "an indispensable part of the process of negotiation." The other major paramilitary organisation, which is associated with the Unionists, broke off contact with the IIC over two years ago, although it was agreed that the commission members were truly non-partisan experts. It took all of seven years of negotiation and nudging to reach this milestone for a single paramilitary organisation, following thirty years fighting. This indicates the significant amount of investment of time and patience that is needed to bring about an end to violence— let alone lasting peace.

Recently in Jamaica, members of the Peace Management Initiative (PMI) team were again in the Mountain View area after another upsurge of violence. They have been there before and they should be prepared to return with adjusted programmes because generations of conflicts will not resolve with a few visits.

The second lesson from Northern Ireland is that where there is a viable, attractive, non-violent option decommissioning is possible. The IRA has put an end to a violent strategy because its members became convinced that it is possible to achieve their ambitions in a more credible fashion. The difficulty with violence in Jamaica is that on the face of it the perpetrators have dubious ambitions. It would be easier to work with individuals and communities under the stress of violence if the killings had some overt political motive. However, far from being dubious, the ambitions of killers in Jamaica, for the most part, like their counterpart in Rio and Johannesburg, are economic. It is difficult to ameliorate these ambitions when the economy, as well as the political will of leaders, is in such a desperate state. The truth is that the depth and breadth of the violence have outstripped the capacity of the country to bring about resolution on its own, in a meaningful time. For the time being, the Jamaican killers remain unconvinced that there is viable, non-violent economic alternative to their desperate strategy of murder and mayhem.

SEXUAL RELATIONS, RAPE, AND CIVIL UNIONS, JUNE 4, 2006

Given a decision that was taken by the Irish Supreme Court recently, it may be prudent that we seek assurance from the Government that our law in Jamaica is not similarly vulnerable. The issue relates to Section 1.1 of the Irish Act of 1935, which governs rape. The Supreme Court accepted the argument that in as much as the law did not allow for any defence to be offered, once intercourse had taken place, the law was inconsistent with constitutional provisions for the right of defence.

The case which brought down the law in question was one in which a boy of 17 had sexual relations with a girl of 14. Under the law, the boy was automatically guilty of rape, since the age of consent is 15. The fact that the girl consented was of no consequence, since under the law she was not of the age to consent—which is why it is called statutory rape. Lawyers for the boy argued, though, that the boy honestly believed that the girl was 16, as she said she was. However, the law denied him the right of defence even though he, in effect, made an honest mistake. The Supreme Court upheld that the law was unconstitutional, which meant that the law had to be repealed.

No Protection

The issue has proven quite embarrassing for the government for a number of reasons. First, suspicions about the constitutionality of the law were raised several months ago because of cases brought before the Supreme Court. The court had in turn invited submissions on the issue, but the Minister of Justice, the Attorney-General and their team seemed to have turned a blind eye or missed the moment, being preoccupied with other less crucial matters. In a discussion paper a few years ago, The Ministry of Justice, Equality and Law Reform referred to the very law as "the bedrock of protection given by the law to girls under 17 years of age." One must then conclude that with the removal of that law, the bedrock of protection for girls under 17 has been removed. No wonder there was a serious outcry, especially from organisations concerned about the protection of children.

Another reason for the embarrassment is that, within a week of the striking down of the law, persons who were incarcerated on the heels of it began appealing their conviction. At the time of this article, the Irish government was appealing the ruling of a case in which a prisoner was released after successfully challenging his incarceration on the basis of the unconstitutional law. It is feared that as many as 12 imprisoned rapists are lining up to make a case for their release on the same basis. The government was hastening to draft legislation to plug the legal loophole.

Sexual Relations and the Law

Our legal luminaries in Jamaica may want to satisfy us that the constitutionality of our law governing statutory rape is fool proof. My suspicion is that the law has not yet been tested on that basis. As far as I am aware also, the discussion on the Charter of Rights has not yet thrown up any question of this nature. It would be a great tragedy if, after knowledge of this unfortunate development, a similar thing were to happen in Jamaica.

While the government is seeking to give us the assurance concerning the strength of our law on statutory rape it may also assure us that it does not intend to go the way of several countries in Europe in legalising sex among early teens. The argument in support of legalising sex among early teens in Ireland is largely predicated on the fact that early teens are involved in sexual activity anyway. A survey in one county revealed that statutory rape is happening all the time, as a large percentage of teenage mothers were involved in sexual relations well before the age of consent. Proponents argue that given the incidence of sexual activity among early teens, the law will not only lower the age of consent but ensure that early teens, whose partners are only two or so years older, need not face prosecution for rape. However, the argument to move towards legalising sexual relations among a certain age group of early teens, simply because it is occurring, will end in absurdity. From that position it will be hard to make a case for outlawing any sexual activity and, in time, any union at all.

Sexual Unions—the Dilemma

The dilemma faced by those who want to proceed on the basis of 'if it is happening then we must legalise it' is similar to the dilemma in which the Government finds itself with respect to the issue of same-sex unions. In a few days hence, lawyers representing a section of the religious community will return to Parliament to urge lawmakers to think carefully about how they proceed in the matter of same-sex unions. If the situation in Ireland is anything to go by, the society must be prepared to make the notion of marriage null and void when one argues that any union between two consenting individuals can, in effect, be treated as a marriage. According to the Irish Justice Minister: "If we are to offer them [same-sex union] something with all the rights and entitlements of a valid marriage, it should also have the same duties attaching to it—indeed, the rights of one partner are often the duties of the other. In effect, it is marriage, albeit by another name."

The serious consequence of this position may only occur to some people when we arrive at a place where we are forced by the logic of present attitudes to relationships to regard the union between two 15-year-old females or males as a formal union. This is not as far-fetched as it seems. Already the link between age of consent for sexual relations and the legal age for proposing cohabitation is being made. Disaster, thou art afoot!

ECONOMIC SUCCESS AND RELIGIOUS AFFILIATION, SEPTEMBER 3, 2006

Recently, a Jamaican delegation went to get first-hand information on the Irish economy, which is probably the best performing economy in Europe—if not the world—to date, this year. The presence and success in Jamaica of Irish-led businesses, like Digicel, have helped to fan the flame of interest in what is happening in Ireland. From this point of view, it is probably not surprising that the Guardian Group also has an Irish national at the helm. Another aspect of the Irish reality that may be of interest to us here in Jamaica is the shifts in its population. I have taken particular interest in how the shift has been affecting the life of the churches and wonder about the connection between economic success and church growth.

In the last decade and a half, the population of the Republic of Ireland has moved from 3.5 million in 1991 to 4.2 million in 2006. Judging by any standard, at a rate of 20 per cent between the two censuses, this is an unusually high rate of increase. Two kinds of migrants, who have been pulled to the state by the very ever-strengthening Irish economy, have been largely responsible for the increase. The first is the return of many Irish citizens, whose families or who themselves went abroad, especially during the 1960s and 1970s. In fact, in 1971 the population was marginally higher that what the population of Jamaica is today. The second set of migrants is a rapid influx of non-Irish immigrants, especially from America, Asia, Africa and Eastern Europe.

Multiculturalism

Many commentators have focussed on what the increase in the population will mean for the social and cultural mix. The rapid adjustment that had to be made to multicultural Ireland is probably the most critical challenge that the nation has had to face since the Great Famine. However, whether there will be a willingness to view the new cultural mix as 'one people,' in a way similar to how Jamaica has tried to define its cultural reality is left to be seen. The recent suggestion that residents who are not citizens should carry ID cards around with them has not gone down well. At worst, it is being seen as a form of xenophobia (fear of strangers) and at best, it is been seen as an attempt to create a two-tier society between the citizens and the others.

There is, however, a set of changes in the area of religious affiliation, which is not getting much attention. It has remained off the radar screen of many observers because they are blinded by the fact that 88.4 per cent of the population still regard themselves as Roman Catholic. The thing to note, though, is that real excitement is happening in the historic and newer Protestant Churches. Take the Anglican (Church of Ireland) for example. When the affiliation moved from 89,000 in 1991 to nearly 116,000 in 2002, it was the first time in 100 years that the census was recording growth in that communion. A little over 90 years ago, the Anglican Communion in the republic was twice the size it is today. The church had been in a continuous state of decline between 1881 and 1991. I am not sure, though, that these figures will comfort the Anglican and Moravian Churches in Jamaica, who themselves, except for the last few years, have been in decline.

The cases of the Methodist Church and Orthodox Church are even more fascinating. Like the Anglican and Presbyterian churches, the Methodists had been declining continuously between 1891 and 1991. However, its affiliation moved from 5,037 in 1991 to 10,033 in 2002. That is an actual change of 99 per cent, which is a much more outstanding way to show the figures than the average change of 6.5 per cent over the period. The increase in Methodism is interesting because it does not appear that that communion is benefiting significantly from the increased migration. In the case of the Orthodox Church, their numbers, due mainly to migration from Eastern Europe, have increased from less than 500 in 1991 to over 10,000 ten years later. The Presbyterians have seen an average increase of about four per cent but their total has, in fact, moved from 13,000 to 20,000 during the 10-year period.

Increasing Pace

By far the most significant changes in terms of religious affiliation among Christians have taken place in the newer Pentecostal and African Instituted Churches. While the numbers in these churches are relatively small, the pace at which they are increasing means that the religious scene in Ireland seems to be moving towards becoming truly plural. In this regard, mention should also be made of the Muslim population, which in a little over 10 years has become the fourth-largest religious body, after the Roman Catholics, the Anglicans and the Presbyterians.

One must then ask about the relationship between economic success and religious affiliation. The question is important because we have traditionally associated rapid increase in religious affiliation with places like Africa and Latin America, where poverty is rife. While there is a marginal increase of those in the state that say they have no religious affiliation, it is amazing that 92.4 per cent of the Irish population still refer to themselves in religious terms. It may be that we have to revise our perception of the role of religion in affluent societies.

APARTHEID IS DEAD, NOT ITS CHILDREN, NOVEMBER 5, 2006

P.W. Botha, former president of the defunct apartheid regime in South Africa, died recently but not many people are grieving for him. Since his name became synonymous with injustice, denial of human rights and all the extremes of racism, it is not surprising that his passing has not overwhelmed the international community with a feeling of grief and loss. Botha's commitment to injustice and the exclusion of blacks from the political process was one of the reasons organisations, like the World Council of Churches (WCC), developed their programmes to combat racism. With the help of the international community, South Africans, inspired by people like Nelson Mandela, slew the apartheid beast, even though its children, segregation and violence, and its parents, injustice and inequality, are still alive and well. No one is singing Botha's praises, but many would be ready to write his epithet: Those who use their power to serve the causes of injustice, state violence and racism will have their day with death and no one will grieve for it.

Appropriate Action

The decade of the 1980s saw apartheid making its most violent kick, after the determination and single-mindedness of the martyrs of the struggle struck the beast with a fatal blow. The ferocity of apartheid in its dying moments led to an unprecedented number of people being killed by the state as one black township after another revolted against its oppression. The scenes we see coming out of Iraq on a daily basis now are reminiscent of the scenes from South Africa. The revolt of the oppressed peoples was described as senseless violence and many of us, from the security of our homes far away, became involved in theoretical discussions about the merit of violence and armed revolt. The financial support of the WCC for the organisations like the African National Congress, (ANC) and the South West Africa People's Organisation (SWAPO), led to a withdrawal of member churches from the council, protesting that the WCC was supporting violence. This is the first lesson from South Africa: when the state uses its army and the police to violently suppress the wishes and rights of the people, violence may be the only appropriate action against the power of the state.

It was in the midst of the growing uncertainty about what actions may be appropriate in response to state-led terror that a group of theologians produced the Kairos Document, which was a theological comment on the political crisis. In the thinking of the authors, it was a kairos, meaning a moment of truth, for apartheid as well as for the churches. One of the ways in which the statement was significant was that it showed leaders stepping back from their situation and making a critical analysis of the situation and the ways their fellow Christians were thinking about it. The authors of the Kairos Document faced the difficulty of having to say to their fellow citizens that their approach to faith and spirituality, in which they moralise about peace, individual conversion, and non-violence was not helping the cry of the masses. They called instead for a proper social analysis to understand the causes of apartheid and the development of a proper political strategy to change the structures of the society. They questioned the attitude in which Christians were sitting and praying for God's intervention but had no vision of the strategy they would engage to move the society out of apathy and paralysis. In so doing, they were bold in exposing the counter-productive nature of the programmes and campaigns that some churches were mounting.

This is the second lesson from South Africa: where society is faced with a crisis, Christian moralising will be of little help. Instead, the churches must avail themselves of proper social analysis and clarify the political strategy they will support for radical change. Those church leaders, who "wax warm" about not becoming involved in politics and that the Christian faith is not about political actions, are fooling themselves. As the Kairos Document was keen to show, the failure to develop appropriate political action will only result in Christians being co-opted into causes that aid and abet injustice.

Regime Credibility

The fundamental issue that apartheid represented was how a regime lost its credibility. For that reason theologians of Kairos Document believed any cooperation with that tyrannical regime was inappropriate. Although that regime has been relegated to the scrap heap of history, its basic moral character remains an issue for nation-states, including our own. It may be easy to see the waning credibility in governments like the Bush and Blair administrations, as they make countless efforts to justify the perpetration of injustice in Iraq. It may not be as easy to see the threat when political parties, as we have in Jamaica, bring their credibility into question by the way in which they receive and use money and the characters with whom they consort.

It may be even more difficult for churches to see that their credibility is called into question by silence, failure to do appropriate social analysis and their ineptitude in not taking appropriate political action. This, too, is a lesson from South Africa: regimes do irreparable damage to their credibility when they persist in justifying wrong.

CRICKET WORLD CUP: PRICED BEYOND THE ORDINARY, FEBRUARY 4, 2007

In just over one month from today, on March 11, to be precise, the 2007 Cricket World Cup, for which we have been preparing for well over four years, will be opened in Trelawny. This world event, which sees the final match being played in Barbados on April 28, is ninth in the series that began at Lord's in 1975. We look forward to the brilliance and we anticipate the rush of adrenaline. It is only a pity my mother, who was an avid cricket fan, is not around to share the laughs with us. Will the record of over 350 runs, which Australia scored in the 2003 finals, be broken? Australia is still the favourites to win, but it is not because Australia has won it three times. By that reckoning the West Indies would be the second favourite, having won it twice. Australia has been the most consistent performer in recent years and should climb to the top of the heap, though we are quite likely to have surprises. The other winners of the competition so far have been India, Pakistan and Sri Lanka.

West Indies, Aussie Showdown

England has appeared in three of the eight finals played. Everyone in the West Indies would be delighted if our team were to win. It would be the sweetest thing to see a showdown with the Aussies in the finals, but by recent performances that is looking quite unlikely, to say the least. When we consider the many millions who will be tuned in, especially to the critical matches and the finals, whether via television, radio, iPod or Internet, the numbers and the associated revenues are mind-boggling. In 2003, over 600,000 attended the 52 matches that were played between the 14 teams. There are 16 teams in this competition, and the International Cricket Council (ICC) expects that this event will be the biggest ever. Indeed, the sizes for the competitions are ever increasing and the broadcast rights for the next two (2011 and 2015), at least, have been sold already. So as world attention is focused on the region for those 47 days, there will be much to see, learn and earn. However, we are just about out of time to make any critical preparation that would add any meaningful value. What's done is done! The final ball is being delivered. We hope that everything will go well, or else dawg nyam wi suppa (i.e we would be in great trouble).

Ticket Sales

The only problem though, is that the event is so beyond the ordinary—the ordinary cricket lover—for I am not sure how many of us will be able to get into the different ovals. If the suggestions on the ICC website are correct, they are now in the final phase of ticket sales, which means premium prices will have to be paid at this point. The prices, which are being offered by one ticketing company, illustrate the beyond-the-ordinariness of this event. For the opening ceremony it will cost a mere €125, which converts to J$10,725 at today's exchange rate. The cheapest tickets remaining are those for the matches between Scotland and the Netherlands, which will be played in St, Kitts/Nevis and New Zealand and Canada, which will be played in St. Lucia. Tickets for both those matches, to be played on March 22, will fetch a mere J$5,480. The cheapest ticket being offered by this company for the West Indies vs Pakistan match on March 13 is J$16,302.

Those who are more able enter the grandstand will do so for a mere J$21,450. Happily, the asking price for the WI vs Zimbabwe on March 19 amounts to only J$8,075. However, unless the ordinary cricket lover takes out a mortgage, he or she will have to settle for watching the final match on TV. The prices being asked to enter Kensington Oval on April 28 range from

J$75,668, that is, seventy-five thousand and mash at the lower end, to J$100,815; that is over one hundred thousand for the grandstand! These prices seemed too unbelievable to be real, so I decided to check the ICC website and registered, as if I was going to buy a ticket. I tried to get a ticket for the Castries and Anse La Raye Stands for the semi-final on Aril 25. Most were sold out, but I could get one for US$130. The cheapest tickets being sold for that same match by the ticketing company I have been looking at was US$190. So, although I could get the ticket for US$60 cheaper directly from the ICC, I felt that at US$130 the price was still beyond the ordinary cricket lover.

Television Coverage

Having gasped at the prices for a while, I concluded that it was better to watch the matches on TV anyway. Why would someone want travel to Barbados to brave the crowds for J$100,000 when all the action can be seen on TV? I shall therefore use the occasion of the matches to go down memory lane reflecting on my prowess—cricketing prowess, of course! Manchester High School cricket team, many moons ago, naturally; Mona's winning cricket team in the inter-campus games played in Barbados 1980, or was it 1982?; inter-hall matches at UWI; the glorious finals of the Leinster Middle Cup in Ireland in 2000. In all these I was actually a player. I have some cricketing pedigree after all. I can do without the crowds and the adrenaline rush. In any case, at those prices, the tickets are not for the ordinary me.

MIGRATING TO IRELAND: PULL FACTORS AND LIMITATIONS, APRIL 1, 2007

It is estimated that 10% of the four million people living in Ireland today are immigrants, some of whom reside permanently. The rapid inward migration that has occurred in the last decade has brought social and demographic changes to the national reality. Last year the economy grew by seven per cent, the most significant growth for the whole European Union. Fears are that the economy will overheat, and a recent fall in the numbers of new houses being sold has given impetus to the speculation that the Celtic tiger has seen the zenith of its performance. Notwithstanding internal anxieties and fears, there are a number of factors that continue to draw migrants to Ireland. A few weeks prior to the increase of Jamaica's national minimum wage in January this year, the Irish government also introduced new minimum wage guidelines for that country. With effect January 1, 2007, the lowest amount any individual can be paid is €5.81per hour. In that case the worker has to be (a student most likely) under 18. (At today's exchange rate €1.00 = JD 90.28.) Once the worker has reached 18 years, (and in the first year of employment), the minimum wage rises to €6.64 per hour. In the second year of employment after eighteen years the minimum wage is €7.47 per hour, which rises to €8.30 for an experienced worker. By way of comparison, the minimum wage in Jamaica is JD80.00 per hour (€0.89), which is about the price of a pack of chewing gum in Ireland. This means that working even at the lowest possible wage, the minimum wage in Ireland is over seven times that of Jamaica.

All National Benefit

Apart from the internationally competitive minimum rate, Ireland has maintained a good welfare system, from which all residents and more particularly all nationals of the European Union benefit. Anything from child benefit to unemployment benefit, childcare allowance and elderly care allowance act as safety nets for the most vulnerable. The relatively high minimum wage and the welfare support are among the reasons for the increasing trends in people, especially from the recent European Union accession states, moving to Ireland. According to the 2006 census, of the 400,000 persons who have taken up residence in the state since 1960, 330,000 (about 82 per cent) took up residence in the last 15 years. Nearly 190,000 persons are said to have taken up residence since 2001. While these are official figures, the word on the street is that the actual numbers are a lot higher.

It is against this background of rapid inward migration that we have to see the recent measures introduced to limit the inflow of migrants. The new strategies of limitation, which came into effect in 2007, consist of two main features. The first is that the government has made having a work permit a requirement for Romanians and Bulgarians, the two most recent members of the European Union, to work in Ireland. Many observers question the wisdom of this decision, as the fact of being members of the European Union means freedom to travel anywhere in the EU. The likely scenario to result from this policy is that a number of migrants from those two recent accession states will enter the low-paid, low-skills job market. Without having the requisite permit to work they will be exploited by employers, who consider employing them jobs a favour.

As we have noticed even with Polish, Lithuanians, and other Eastern Europeans who do not need work permits, the fear of losing their jobs causes them to endure much abuse and the trampling of their rights. Moreover, though the legislation is there to protect the workers, the government is reticent in going after employers who are flouting the law. If this can happen with migrant workers who do not need a permit to work, it boggles the mind to try and imagine the abuse Romanians and Bulgarians will suffer. In recent noteworthy cases, which are being termed human trafficking, Romanians paid up €1,000 each to unscrupulous persons, who gave them assurances of finding them jobs, only to be dumped in the state with the traffickers disappearing without a trace.

Green Card System

The second feature of the limitation strategies is the implementation of a Green Card system in the new work permit regime. Under the new regime, which came into effect on February 1, 2007, Green Cards will be issued to those migrant workers who have been offered jobs with remuneration of €60,000.00 or above. These jobs need not be advertised but must be for at least a two-year contract. Spouses may accompany the Green Card holders and will be allowed to work without the need for a work permit. Permit to work will also be given to migrant workers who will be paid between €30,000 and €60,000, providing there is no European national who can be found to fill the position. Only in exceptional cases will permit be given for job paying under €30,000.00.

To further reinforce the limitation, under the new legislation certain occupations do not qualify for permit. These include clerical and administrative, general operatives and labourers, operations and production staff, sales representatives, hotel and tourism workers and skilled workers associated with the building industry. In other words, the government has determined that there are sufficient persons already present in the country, available from the older EU member states, to fill these positions.

Serious Difficulties

Even with its economic development, Ireland is not a likely spot for Jamaican migration. Of the 50,000 permits issued between 2005 and 2006, only 25 went to Jamaicans. Migrants from the Philippines, Brazil, India, China, South Africa and Eastern Europe account for the majority of migrant workers. However, there are several Jamaicans living in the state, some of whom travelled on exchange programmes. Conversations with some of the exchange students reveal that many have had serious difficulties finding proper accommodation and the necessary jobs to cover their living expenses. Local officers of the exchange programmes should update themselves on the situation in Ireland, which is changing rapidly, so that they can prepare students more effectively for working and studying in Ireland.

In the present climate, Jamaicans seeking to work in Ireland will be met with many obstacles. Apart from the stringent visa requirements, there are serious biases against competing for jobs in the labour market. This is also true for all job seekers from outside the EU, with the exception of America. It is for that reason, as recent research has shown, that migrant workers are, by and large, more qualified than their Irish counterparts working at the same level. Many highly competent workers from India, China, the Philippines and Russia are working in jobs for which they are far too qualified.

The best chance nowadays of settling in Ireland, without a hassle, is to secure a position which can pay a salary of €60,000.00 and above. Many such public jobs are often advertised on www.publicjobs.ie. Direct contact with companies in the different chambers of commerce would be another route. Experienced professionals, especially in the medical and technical fields, should also try their luck at competing for positions in the €30,000–€60,000 bracket. The websites www.monster.ie, www.loadzajobs.ie and www.jobs.ie are some of the better known ones. People who do not qualify for permits hoping to work in the job categories mentioned above will most definitely face serious difficulties.

Chapter Three

Faith and the Church

THE CHURCH'S INFLUENCE ON EMANCIPATION, AUGUST 3, 2003

When we think of Emancipation today, people often think of the positive role played by local churches. This perception of the influence of the church is due in part to the perception of the planters of the early 19th century. In their minds, the missionaries working among the people were responsible for the series of rebellion and revolt, which preceded the 1834 Act of Emancipation. The Moravian Church was the first to have begun missionary work among the people kept as slaves and was already 80 years in Jamaica at the time of Emancipation. However, the way they perceived the influence of the local churches on Emancipation and how they were perceived by the planters, has not been as much the subject of attention. Writing at the time of the centenary celebrations, 20 years after the Act was promulgated, J.H. Buckner, who was then minister of the Moravian Church at Fairfield, noted that the Baptists and Methodists ministers were loudly accused of being instigators. Moravian missionaries, he said were likewise suspected and openly accused by the planters and the House of Assembly of having occasioned discontent and insurrection. The private conversations (Speaking, as they came to be known), which the missionaries held with the slaves, were especially obnoxious to the proprietors, and they accused the Moravian brethren of using these to instil evil disposition into the minds of the people. [Buckner, The Moravians in Jamaica, 1854]

Likewise, the people who were kept slaves seemed to have been of the general impression that the change that eventually came in their condition was to be ascribed to the influence of the Gospel and the labours of the missionaries [Buckner, 115]. In one instance at New Eden, near Bogue in St.

Elizabeth, the missionary reported how a Negro insisted that it was not Jesus but the missionaries themselves who helped them to be free. When the day of Emancipation came, thousands went to worship as a way to mark the occasion. At the Zorn Moravian Church in Christiana, Manchester, there were several services on the same day, as the building was not able to hold the thousands that went out to worship. The consequence of this association between the Gospel and freedom was that after Emancipation the churches expanded at a remarkable rate. Between 1831 and 1837, the Moravians experienced a 100 per cent rise in membership. Then between 1836 and 1843 the Moravians alone built no fewer than 13 [primary] schools. The rate of expansion among the Baptists and the Methodists was equally impressive. At Maidstone in Manchester and Darliston in Westmoreland in particular, the Moravians purchased lands, which they made available to the ex-slaves at greatly reduced cost. This was an important intervention by the church, given the rapacious attitude of the planters who were keen to recover from the earnings lost as a consequence of Emancipation.

However, the missionaries of the local churches did not readily own the influence the church is believed to have had in the rebellions and uprisings that preceded Emancipation. In general, missionaries were keen to be seen as not disrupting the status quo. So the church leadership was keen to maintain the social status because in that way they were assured a preaching post, free from official harassment.

Exposing Social Defects

As it is today, so it was then, the preaching of non-violence and obedience to authorities and the desire to avoid public disruption functioned as a serious inertia against any attempt to expose instances of social injustice. As it is now, so it was then – the people involved in violence bear the cost of the social injustice and exclusion, upon which violence is constructed. As it was in the 1820s and 1830s, we are not willing today to admit that violence - for example in Mountain View - is an attempt to expose the critical social defects in the 'under-belly' of the society.

The role of the churches in establishing schools, thus setting the base for the country's public education system is indeed critical. By facilitating the acquisition of land to mitigate the extreme cost the planters were charging for rent, the church also set the basis for land ownership in the social underclass. However, the desire of the missionaries to avoid social disruption and their denial of any link between the gospel imperative and Emancipation means the influence of the church on Emancipation was unintended. Therefore, the perception that the churches played an important positive role in Emancipation is a somewhat default benefit to them today.

The churches then cannot afford to be triumphalist about that perception, as if it remains forever relevant and true. Rather, it is a challenge for the churches to verify that they are significant forces for social transformation by attending to the extensive social injustice and dislocation that are evident in the society today.

INTERFAITH RELATIONS, OCTOBER 5, 2003

A few years ago the Governor General, Sir Howard Cooke, proclaimed that October 2 each year should be observed as interfaith day. It is clear, however, that the religious community in Jamaica has not taken cognisance of this proclamation. In this article I want to put forward some ideas relating to the issue of interfaith relations under the heading of religious pluralism, to get a conversation going between representatives of the different religious communities.

The Rise of Theologies of Pluralism

The second half of the 20th century has witnessed a concerned attempt among Christian theologians in the West to come to terms with the growing incidence of religious pluralism. The recognition that the claims of other religions could no longer be overlooked in Christian theological discourse was an inevitable development from the undercutting of traditional claims to Christian authority, which was achieved principally during the Enlightenment period (about the years 700-1800), where rationalism emerged as the pre-eminent basis for adjudicating between truth claims.

However, in addition to the levelling effect of the Enlightenment on religion, there were two other factors that hastened the drive to develop a viable theology of religious pluralism. One was the result of missionary enterprises that took place in the previous two centuries. Much to the consternation of the missionaries, the religious worlds of Hinduism, Buddhism and Islam, in particular, were not caves of error and ignorance as it was construed in the initial missionary thrust. What the missionaries found, mainly in Asia and Africa, was that these religious traditions were sustaining the lives of millions of people and seemed impervious to Christian evangelism.

In 1887, speaking at the Centennial Anniversary of the Moravian Society for Propagating of the Gospel, Rev. Morris Leibert shared that "Asia continues to be a stronghold of systems and beliefs whose worth and strength must be acknowledged." Sixty years later when writing about the difficulty in propagating the gospel in Suriname, one Moravian missionary that their mission work has not made any appreciable progress among these British Indians. Two trends were said to be observed: there are pious Mohammedans or Hindus who reject Christianity, either because they consider themselves superior to it or because they see no difference between Christianity and Mohammedanism.

The realisation of the internal strength and cohesion of the other religions led early 19th century theologians and missionaries to plead for justice, courtesy and love when dealing with the other religions. Theologians, for example Frederick Maurice (1805-1872), began to argue that the encounter with other religious traditions might even offer correctives to Christian theological formulations. The theologies of pluralism that developed have built on this earlier awareness.

The other factor that has affected religious attitudes in the West is the rapid increase in the presence of other religious traditions in the metropolitan areas of Europe and North America, as a result of increased emigration towards the end of the colonial era. Every major city in Europe and North America is home to thousands of people of other faiths. Encountering people of other religious traditions is not the esoteric privilege of missionaries afield but a day to day reality for the ordinary Christian.

The Caribbean itself is a melting pot of all kinds of African, Asian, European, American and Caribbean religious expressions. In a real sense, the theologies of pluralism that developed were aimed at giving theological content to the de facto plural approach that people were already taking to their religious faith. On one hand, they were seeking, to justify the openness and tolerance with which Christians approached people of other faiths, or on the other hand, they were seeking to remind Christians that the uniqueness of the Christian faith should not be compromised in the interest of good relations among neighbours.

Approaches to Pluralism

In seeking to come to terms with the new reality of religious pluralism then, a number of approaches have been developed. Formerly the approaches were referred to as exclusive, inclusive and pluralist. However, these designations have proven to be somewhat inaccurate. Today, the approaches can be organised into three main types. One is the approach that favours a commitment to other religions. This approach calls attention to the difficulty of adjudicating between religious truth claims and consequently sees the religions as being virtually on par. The other approach is one that favours a commitment to one's own tradition.

This approach seeks to take seriously the questions that other faiths put to the Christian faith but sees the Christian faith as being the most plausible.

A third approach, which essentially is situated between the two approaches mentioned above, is called the cultural-linguistic approach. This approach treats the religious tradition as one would a language or a culture, where the doctrines are seen as communally authoritative rules of discourse. There is a refusal here to pass judgement on the other religions because each is unique in its own way.

Each approach has its own weaknesses, especially in relation to the question of whether all religions can be the locus of divine revelation. They also fail to deal adequately with the issue of the doctrine of Christ, which is of fundamental importance in the relationship between Christianity and the other religions.

It seems though, that the big challenge we face is to be able to decide which religion is least responsible for perpetuating violence and hatred of others. As we consider the meaning of interfaith day, Christians in Jamaica are challenged to re-think the attitudes we have to people of other faiths, bearing in mind that it may not be possible to achieve peace in Jamaica until there is a commitment to change the language we use when referring to others who may not share of values and beliefs.

KNOWLEDGE-BASED ECONOMY AND THE CHURCH, JANUARY 2, 2004

As we enter this New Year 2004, one of the issues facing the churches is how to respond to the challenges of a knowledge-based economy. It seems to me that this is an important issue because there is growing agreement that we must understand the emerging regional economy as one based on the ability to create, store and sell knowledge. The Summit of the Americas, which was held in Quebec, Canada in 2001, already arrived at this consensus. According to the Final Declaration, a new economy is emerging, which is "defined by a vastly enhanced capacity to access knowledge and improve flows of information." It is safe to say that that new economy has arrived.

Strategy for Coping with a Knowledge-Based Economy

The declaration also noted that connectivity is the most effective way in which the region can respond to the challenges of this new economy. Connectivity refers to the creation of linkages between the governments and peoples of the region, designed to maximise the possible gains from the emerging economy. The capitalist ethic of competition is evident in the new economy, given the increasing emphases on speed, power and memory capacity. This is seen, for example, in the types of computers and digital equipment that are coming on the market. What we are having, then, is an expansion of the logic of capitalism to formally include the acquisition and sale of knowledge. Whereas the commodities in the early capitalist economies were goods and services, the commodity in the knowledge-based economy is knowledge itself. The speed, at which we create and access knowledge, as well as the capacity for storing, distributing and using it efficiently, is the imperative of this new economy.

It remains the case that knowledge is power. Connectivity is a strategy to ensure broad-based benefits in a capitalist economy. This conception of the immediate future is already shaping our thinking and has begun to influence the solutions that we propose to deal with regional problems. It means that whether or not the churches agree that the future (in fact the present!) has to do with how knowledge is managed, they will have to deal with the future in those terms. There is, then, a theological challenge for the churches, when the task of participating effectively in the emerging society is construed as a vastly enhanced capacity to access knowledge.

The Story of Anti-Ecumenism

Connectivity, in the form of ecumenical partnership, which was a potent idea in the churches 30 to 40 years ago, saw the birth of the ecumenical institutions of the region. In fact, the idea of a Council of Churches was discussed in Jamaica from the early 1920s. The United Theological College of the West Indies was formed in mid 1960s. The Caribbean Conference of Churches was formed in the 1970s and other ecumenical groupings in Jamaica were formed in the 1980s. Conversely, the last decade has witnessed a weakening of ecumenical relations as churches fall back into the shells of their respective traditions, in order to resist the threat of the loss of identity that globalisation has caused.

At the same time, also, an increasing number of churches have been born that respond directly to the need for uniqueness and certitude. Two characteristics of these newer churches are (a) the effective use they make of the electronic media and the Internet and (b) their anti-ecumenical posture. These churches have already bought into the definition of knowledge as a commodity and are truly products of the new economy. Having their counterparts in the other religions (especially Islam and Hinduism), these religious fundamentalists have experienced faster numerical growth then the churches at the more liberal end of the religious spectrum. The newer churches and religious movements have accepted the description of society as knowledge-based but they seem to have rejected the notion of connectivity, as a religious strategy. In this respect the churches have mastered the ideal of capitalism, which is about using the facilities of the economy to maximise the growth of the "firm." There is emerging, however, an uncomfortable nexus between anti-ecumenism and growth.

The Rejection of Connectivity

Therefore, although there is recognition that connectivity is a way in which the region can respond to the challenges of a knowledge-based society, the churches are moving in an opposite direction. In other words, there is suspicion about the virtues of connectivity and ecumenical partnership. The decline in the effectiveness of national and regional ecumenical bodies suggests that the churches need to resolve the question of how they will work together in the new situation. In a certain sense the experience of the churches prefigure the experience of the countries of the region, as they try to come to terms with the new knowledge-based market. The prolonged discussion as to whether or not we should have a regional court of appeal, for example, is the political counterpart of the anti-ecumenism and anti-connectivity among the churches.

The immediate future for the Americas seems to be one in which those that have the means to exploit the knowledge-based economy will grow while those that are slow in getting their capacity developed will be left behind, The issue that churches and indeed the nations of the region must then face, is the question of what strategy they will adopt if there is no truth to the assertion that connectivity is a critical means for coping effectively m this knowledge- based economy.

THE FIRST PROTESTANT DENOMINATION IN JAMAICA: ITS ADVENT AND CHARACTER, DECEMBER 8, 2004

It was during the Advent season of 1754 that the first Protestant denomination arrived in Jamaica. The year 2004 is therefore 250 years since the Moravian Church began its witness in Jamaica. The church will observe a year-long 250th anniversary celebration, beginning with a Provincial Day of Prayer on December 9 and followed by the grand opening service at the Bethlehem Moravian College on December 12. Only two other denominations in Jamaica, the Roman Catholic (1492) and the Anglican (1655), have passed this 250 years milestone. Having been established in Moravia, Czechoslovakia in 1457 as the first Protestant Church (60 years before the Lutheran Reformation), the Moravian Church also became the first Protestant Church to be established in the Caribbean (St. Thomas, 1732 and Jamaica, 1754). Whatever may be said of the denomination, its work in Jamaica coincides with just about half the period of Jamaica's recorded history. Any reflection on the period 1754-2004 is at the same time a reflection on an important segment of the nation's life.

Ecumenical Modesty

The Moravians have concentrated their witness mostly in the southern parishes. There are a few congregations in parishes of Kingston and St. Andrew, two each in Clarendon and St. James and one each in St. Catherine and St. Ann. Apart from these, the other 60 congregations are located in Manchester, St. Elizabeth and Westmoreland. One of the questions people often ask is how is it that the denomination has been in Jamaica for such a long time and has not expanded beyond these parishes? However, this character of its work is the result of a conscious decision of the early 19th century not to venture in areas that were being served by other churches, particularly the Baptists, who were at the time located mostly in the eastern and northern parishes. Younger Moravians today believe the church may have remained far too long in this paradigm of ecumenical modesty. They argue that if the church were less concerned with avoiding competition in the mission field, it may well have situated itself in each parish, since it had the conviction of being in possession of a credible Christian witness.

Preferential Option

The decision to establish work in Jamaica was specifically to work among the slaves, as a result of which collaboration with the planters was necessary. It was nearly 80 years before, that the Moravians cut the umbilical knot between themselves and the planters. In 1831, leaders of the church decided to relocate their chapel at Mesopotamia, near Frome in Westmoreland, to be "an independent station free from the embarrassments consequent of being restricted to [the] estate." [Minutes of the Mission Conference held at Fairfield, 1831] The financial fortunes (or misfortunes!) of the Moravian Church may be related to the fact that for 140 years after its establishment, the church remained altogether in the rural areas. This rural focus was also the result of a conscious decision to work in the hilly country areas where the slaves and later ex-slaves lived.

Large Gathering

In any case, the Anglican Church, then Church of England, was located in each parish capital, and consistent with its ecumenical modesty the church did not consider it a real necessity to be in the towns. The first Moravian Church to be established in a town was the Church of the Redeemer (1893), which was first located at 23-25 Hanover Street and subsequently relocated at the corner of North and Duke Streets. Perhaps the earliest large gathering of Moravians in a major township was in 1832 when a group came up from Bogue, St. Elizabeth, to Mandeville, as witnesses in the trial of the Rev. Henrich Pfeiffer, who was arrested and charged for instigating revolts among the slaves. Pfeiffer was eventually freed and, although the early Moravian leaders tried to assert their non-involvement in slave revolts, it was always the perception of the committee of the House of Assembly investigating the matter that the Moravians were to share the blame.

This perception was justified because the Moravians themselves admitted at their Conference at New Eden (Bogue) later in 1832, that "some of our members were engaged in the rebellion, though without committing any acts of outrage. Several of the properties in Manchester, on which majority of the Negroes are in connection with us, were among those that struck work. Since then, there has been a very thin attendance and, in general, the state of the congregation is very mournful." (Minutes of the Mission Conference, held at New Eden in 1832) As a result of the charge of the House of Assembly and out of fear of the call in the papers for the Moravian chapels to be destroyed, the practice of meeting members for speaking (private consultation) and instruction for membership was discontinued for some time.

Social Transformation

For financial reasons, the primary school, run by the Redeemer Moravian Church on North Street, was closed in 1898, only a few years after inception. The other congregations established in Kingston and St. Andrew have not established primary schools, but have opted for vocational and medical outreach ministries. On the other hand, the congregations in the rural areas are, for the most part, associated with primary schools. Some 40 of the primary schools originally established by the church are still in operation today, 27 of which are Moravian denominational schools.

The link with education was not accidental, but arose from two important convictions inherited from John Amos Comenius (d.1670), the Czechoslovakian-born Bishop of the Moravian Church, who is called the 'Father of Modern Education'. One conviction is that educating the mind is a divine imperative, because it is one of the arenas of God's revelation.

The second is that education is the surest means to banish darkness and disharmony from the world. The Moravian Church remains convicted today that the only way to put the menace of crime effectively to rest in our nation is through effective education. For the church, it was anathema to consider evangelism separate from social transformation. The numerical size of the church after 250 years may be due to its preoccupation with social transformation at the expense of evangelistic mission. Alternatively, it seems to have treated social transformation as evangelism. It will be interesting to see whether, with this approach to mission, there will be a Moravian Church in Jamaica 250 years from now in 2254.

MORAVIANS IN WIDER SOCIETY, MARCH 31, 2005

In recognition of the role of the Church in the wider context of the Jamaican society, the congregation of the 69th Moravian Synod will host a public session on 'The Church in the Caribbean Single Market Economy' today at 7:00 p.m. at Golf View Hotel in Mandeville. Presenters will include Senator Delano Franklin, State Minister of Foreign Affairs; the Reverend Dr. Roderick Hewitt, Moderator of the United Church in Jamaica and Grand Cayman, the Reverend Gerard Granado, General Secretary of the Caribbean Conference of Churches and the Reverend Stanley Clarke, former President of the Jamaica Council of Churches.

Re-examining Relationships

As Moravians observe 250 years of existence in Jamaica, under the theme, Re-kindling the Flame' the Church is redefining its identity and mission against the background of a number of developments at international, regional and national levels. According to the Rev. Dr. Livingstone Thompson, president of the Provincial Elders' Conference, the Moravian Church cannot continue to exist without involvement in the social issues that are transforming the wider society and arc affecting the quality of life of its members. He said that Moravians have had to re-examine the Relationship between the Church and the rest of the society. The changes in international trade have had a negative impact on the production and sale of sugar and banana, with the consequence being that the viability of these industries cannot be guaranteed.

The move towards the formulation of the Caribbean Single Market and Economy (CSME) is expected to have a positive impact on the movement of goods and services in the region. He noted that trade issues and recurring natural disasters in the region have challenged the Moravian community in the Caribbean to develop a comprehensive response strategy. Thompson said that the Moravian Provinces in the region are under an imperative to strengthen their levels of collaboration, in order to make a more effective contribution to the regional process.

Significant Impact

The Moravian movement in Jamaica has had a significant impact on the establishment of institutions in the areas of education, youth development, health, the media and religion. At the national level, the Moravian community is urging government to develop a multi-sectoral approach to defuse the debilitating effect of crime and violence on national life. Along with traditional policing, the Church is calling for the development of employment opportunities particularly for young people.

The 69th Synod is also reaffirming the Church's commitment to strengthen its lobby against the development of a gaming industry in Jamaica. Also of concern to the Synod will be the global issues of HIV/AIDS, the 'war on terror', the promulgation of policies which threaten the rights and freedom of persons in the region and the Tsunami disaster. These issues have also challenged the Moravia community to formulate a clear strategy to respond to international disasters. The five-day synod ends tomorrow with the election of officers of the governing Provincial Elders' Conference, the executive board of the Moravian Church. Rev. Dr Thompson will not seek re-election.

THE BISHOPS OF ROME AND THE ANTI-POPES, APRIL 8, 2005

Pope John Paul II, who is known otherwise as Karol Wojtyla, served for 27 years, five years less than Pius IX, who was the longest serving pontiff (1846-1878). The recent death of this first Slav pope is an interesting moment to reflect on the office of the Bishop of Rome. The imminent election of his successor reminds us that moments like this in the life of the Roman Catholic Church have been moments of conflict and contention. One of the outcomes of those contentious moments was the election of what in official Roman Catholic history is called anti-popes. The expression anti-pope means bishops of Rome who were elected while an elected pontiff was in office or bishops that were elected not in accordance with canon law. The aim of this article is to look briefly at some of the anti-popes and the fighting and the power struggle that was behind their election and demise.

Of the 308 bishops of Rome (note that the apostle Peter is not included in this listing), 38 of them have been designated anti-pope. Of course, the difference between earlier periods and now is that there is no obvious imperial or political interest in who is elected pope. It is also true that, as it was then, and so it is now, the cardinals themselves are not always at one in every single issue, but their differences are more carefully managed away from public scrutiny.

First Bishop of Rome

The convention of calling Peter the Apostle the first Bishop of Rome, and hence the first pope, dates back to the late second century, although the title of pope is believed to have been used for the first time during the bishopric of Siricius (c.384-c. 1399). [Michael Baigent and Richard Leigh, The Inquisition, 2000]. However, the earliest list for the succession of bishops of Rome mentions Linus as the first bishop. From the earliest extant accounts, it is more accurate to say then that Linus (c.66-c.78) was the first bishop of Rome. According to respected church historian, J.N.D. Kelly, the monarchical episcopate began emerging during the bishopric of Telesphorus, who was bishop in Rome C.125-C. 136. [Oxford Dictionary of Popes, 1996]

First African Pope

Of interest to persons in Africa and the African diaspora is the question of who was the first African pope. According to the Liber Pontificalis, (ed. Duchesne, Paris, 1886-92), which is the Roman Catholic official listing of bishops, the first listed African-born pope was Victor I, who was bishop of Rome from 189 to 198 CE. In was during his bishopric that the current practice of celebrating Easter on the Sunday following the Jewish Passover (14th Nissan) was introduced. Victor invoked the wrath of the Eastern Church by excommunicating those who held to the practice of observing Easter on 14th Nissan.

The Anti-Popes

Although there is a difference of opinion in modern research about who the anti-popes are, it is generally held that it was during the bishopric of Callistus I, (c.217- Sc.22) that the first anti-pope Hippolytus emerged. The concern of Hippolytus was that Bishop Callislus I was misguided in his theology and lax in his discipline. A group of schismatics elected Hippolytus as alternative bishop. The schism it caused continued until close to his death in 235CE. Shortly before his death, while in exile on Sardinia, the notorious Island of Death, Hippolytus denounced his claim to be bishop and was restored.

The second anti-pope, Novation, was the chief spokesperson among the priest during the period 249-251CE. During this period, there was no election for the bishop of Rome due to the persecution that the Church was experiencing. That would not be the only time that the Roman Church existed without a bishop in Rome because later, in the period 253-260CE, presbyters led the church for about two years. Novation was surprised that Cornelius received the nod over him at the election and so mounted an offensive objecting to this unprecedented move and eventually threw Felix II out of the city. Felix II had enough support from among committed members and the clergy to remain in a strong position in the outskirts of the city up to the time of his death in 365CE. It was not long after, 366 to be exact, that there was yet another schism, in which Ursinus was elected. Soon after his election, there was another election by the Felix II supporters, who were the more numerous. They elected Damascus, who, with the support of the city officials, gained the upper hand in a bloody street fight and exiled Ursinus. The tensions between the supporters of Ursinus and the recognised bishop of Rome continued until the death of Damascus in 384CE, when another bishop was decisively elected.

The death of Zosimus on December 26, 418 sparked yet another controversy. A group of deacons and presbyters elected Eulalius on December 27, 418 and a larger group of presbyters elected Boniface two days later. The matter was further complicated by the emperor's recognition of both persons. In a bid to settle the dispute, both men were asked to leave the city and to allow the bishop of a neighbouring See to preside at the Easter services of 419. Eulalius, however, returned and by force took up occupation in the Lateran basilica. The subsequent publication of an imperial edict led to his expulsion from Rome and the formal recognition of Boniface. In each of the subsequent centuries between 500 and 1100, there was at least one papal schism that led to the election of an anti-pope.

The Eleven Anti-Popes

The period between 1100 and 1179 was by far the one that witnessed the greatest struggle for papal power. During these 79 years, there were as many as 11 anti-popes, including Celestine II who, though canonically elected, was neither consecrated nor enthroned. It is said that as soon as he was elected troops entered the assembly and forced him to resign. The anti-pope Honorius was installed in his place. J. N. D Kelly believes that the fighting between the families reflected a tension within the community of Cardinals, some of whom wanted the church to move towards renewal and a constructive engagement with the imperial power, hence the election of Celestine II.

The forced installation of Honorius II was, on that score, evidence of the resurgence of the old guard, who wanted to maintain distance from the political directorate. This would not be the last time in that century that force would be used to install a pontiff. Probably the most outstanding for that century was the forced installation, in 1159, of Victor IV (the second anti-pope by that designation in the century), who was supported by the imperialist cardinals. His installation, which was supported by the Emperor, led to a schism between church and state that lasted nearly twenty years. The tension between the emperor and the cardinals led to the succession of several anti-popes being elected and installed with imperial support.

The Last of the Anti-Popes

The 15th century was another year of severe stress for the Roman Catholic Church, for in that year papal schism saw the election of five anti-popes by the middle of the century. The Great Schism, which lasted for nearly 40 years, reached its climax at the Council of Constance (1414-18). In many ways this was a council called to bring about unity in the Roman Catholic

Church. Two perceived threats to its unity were (a) the preaching of the Reformer John Hus, from whose followers the Moravian Church (Unitas Fratrum) later sprung and (b) concurrent existence of three popes. With the election of Martin V at the Council of Constance, the days of the Great Schism drew to a close because the rival popes accepted the decision of the Council. The last of the anti-popes was Felix V, who was declared spurious because it was one cardinal and 32 persons named by the commission of Council of Basle which elected him (in 1449). This was one of those times when the person elected pope was a layman. Amadeus, who was consecrated Felix V, was a rich businessman, well respected for his piety. Through the diplomacy of the Pope Nicholas V, who was elected in 1447, Felix eventually abdicated. In return he was given a substantial pension and the episcopal duties over a large area in Switzerland.

Papal Excesses

As extreme as the excesses of the antipopes were, they pale into insignificance to some excesses of the papacy in the period between mid-15th and mid-16th century. The popes of the 15th century were for the most part involved in wars against the Muslims nations or in conflicts in Europe. They spared no effort in seeking to crush attempts at reform or secular thinking. Being often drawn from influential Italian families [Alister E. McGrath, Reformation Thought, 2000], the pontiffs used their influences to aggrandise themselves and close family members. In the view of some observers, the papacy reached its lowest ebb during the 16th, 17th and 18th centuries, as the bishops of Rome tried to negotiate their way through the periods of the Renaissance and Enlightenment. A good example of papal excesses can be found in Leo X, who was made Bishop of Rome in 1513, being only 37 years of age, having been made cardinal at age 13. Through his extravagance, the papacy was thrown into serious debt. According to one historian, Leo was a devious and double-tongued politician and an inveterate nepotist.

The Future of the Papacy

Given the excesses of the papacy over the years, it is amazing that the 1st Vatican Council (1869-70) should have adopted the doctrine of papal infallibility. According to this doctrine, when the pope speaks ex cathedra, that is, when as chief pastor he defines a doctrine of faith or moral to be held by the whole church, he is infallible. The irony of this declaration is that it was made at the same time the pope was denouncing the view that the pope can or should reconcile himself to or agree with progress, liberalism and modern civilisation. According to Baigent and Leigh, by this attitude towards the modern world the pope desired God to abrogate and annul the 19th century in its entirety. The doctrine of infallibility was seen as the papal attempt to usurp the divine prerogative.

The issuing of the doctrine of infallibility coincided with a rising tide of anti-clericalism, which accounts for the development of different forms of religious life being led by the laity. From its earliest promulgation to today, the doctrine of infallibility has caused problems for the church. For more than a year after its promulgation the bishops of Hungary refused to accept the ruling of the council. The future of the papacy will be linked to how this doctrine of infallibility is used. According to the Roman Catholic theologian, Hans Kung, rather than speaking of the infallibility of the pope, the council should have spoken of the church as being indefectible. In Kung's view, the papal claim to infallibility still remains the central and most difficult obstacle to all union-efforts with the Roman Catholic Church. [Hans Kung, et al, Toward Vatican III: The Work that Needs to be Done, 1978].

It is nearly 600 years since the last antipope. For the sake of the Roman Catholic Church and for the whole Christian community, one can only hope that when the announcement is made a few days hence, it will not precipitate the controversies in the past that gave rise to the election of antipopes. The wider Christian community should also hope that the election of the new pontiff of the Roman Catholic Church would revise this notion of papal infallibility.

HAPPY NEW YEAR MY FOOT!
JANUARY 1, 2006

Since Midnight last night, the expression 'Happy New Year' would have been said and heard over and over again. We will hear it for a few more weeks this month, after which it will disappear until December, when it will be preceded by the expression, "We wish you a merry Christmas." Don't be surprised if in saying 'Happy New Year' to someone you get the response, "Happy New Year my foot!" The fact is that the expression stirs negative emotions in many people. However, there are different ways to look at this expression, though to my mind only one of those ways really makes sense.

In the first place, people use this expression as a greeting, in the same way people say 'compliments of the season'. For them there is no particular meaning behind the saying. It is the way of saying hello in early January. It is to January what 'bless you' is to a sneeze. It is an occasional expression that simply fills a void when there is nothing else to say. It is a verbal fashion that is analogous to wearing red during Christmas to match the leaves of the red poinsettia. For these people, 'Happy New Year', might well be 'Happy ground hog day'. It is just something people say. It is neither indicative of any particular belief about happiness nor any particular philosophy of time.

When 'Happy New Year' is simply a greeting, its non-use subtracts nothing from the value or meaning of life and its use only adds words. However, if we regard its use as more than merely using words, then it is more than just a 'hello', which leads to the second way in which we might understand the saying 'Happy New Year'.

A Sincere Wish

'Happy New Year' is a sincere wish that the year brings happiness. As wishful thinking, it is a suggestion that our fortunes are 'in the stars' and that all we can do is to wish that the coming events will work out in our favour. Many people in fact live with this kind of captivity to the horoscope, biting their nails and crossing their fingers in the hope that the crystal ball will bring them good news; that the dice will bring them good luck. In principle there is nothing bad about wishing someone good luck. However, while it is one thing to recognise that we can't control certain events, it is quite another thing to try to wish problems away or to try to wish happiness into being. Experience has taught us that the things that work against our happiness are not affected by good wishes. If good wishes could make a real difference to the crime and poverty that are threatening to overwhelm us, for example, then we would all be 'grinning teeth'. Therefore, as civil as it might be to wish someone a happy New Year, we must admit that it smacks of hollowness, unless, of course, we are prepared to add something else to our good wishes. This brings us to another way in which to understand saying 'Happy New Year'.

Thirdly, 'Happy New Year' may be understood as a benediction, which is the only use that really makes sense to me. The word benediction comes from the Latin root, benedicere, which means to bless. Church goers would be familiar with the different forms of blessing that the presiding minister pronounces on the congregation at the end of the service. The most popular benediction in the Old Testament is to be found in Numbers 6:24-26: "The Lord bless you and keep you; the Lord make his face to shine on you and be gracious to you; the Lord lift up his countenance upon you and give you his peace." The one most popular from the New Testament is found in 2 Corinthians 13:14: "The grace of our Lord Jesus Christ, and the Love of God, and the communion of the Holy Spirit be with you all."

More Than Words

When these benedictions are pronounced, they are more than words and they are certainly not wishful thinking. Rather, the benediction is a prayer being offered to God for the one on whom the blessing is pronounced. If we understand 'Happy New Year' as a benediction, then it carries with it the implication that happiness is a divine quality. Moreover, by pronouncing the blessing of a happy new year on someone, it implies that there is a connection of duty between the one pronouncing the blessing and the one who is the recipient. In other words, as benediction, 'Happy New Year' recognises that the one who is speaking makes a commitment to contribute to the happiness of the other. Now this is where we run into unavoidable difficulty because by this we propose to connect our words to our deeds.

How can we pronounce the benediction of a happy new year and then work to ensure that others will have an unhappy one? It means that as individuals, firms, committees and boards of institutions we cannot afford to be mindless or naïve about the consequences of our decisions, which might cause untold unhappiness for others and lead to a truly unhappy year. Happy New Year to you!

IN THE BEGINNING, GOD, APRIL 2, 2006

"I want to begin by recognising . . . Almighty God." This is how the Most Hon. Portia L. Simpson Miller, Prime Minister, began her address at her swearing-in ceremony last Thursday. The PM has been open in expressing her faith in God. Her boldness in calling us to centre our thoughts on God is really her first prime ministerial challenge to the nation. It reminds us of the former Governor General who, in his role as head of state, trumpeted the cause of Christ and patronised interfaith conversation. I am sure it has warmed the hearts of the religious public to see PM Simpson-Miller starting on such a footing. She can guarantee that there will be no reluctance to pray for her in church.

The self-understanding of Jamaica, as a nation under God, is indicated by words of the National Anthem, 'Eternal Father bless of land', and the National Pledge, 'Before God and all mankind.' It is also true to say that our political leaders have had no reason to apologise for the references they make to God when they address the nation. Both the GG and the former PM ended their speech last Thursday with reference to God. So, in a sense PM Simpson Miller is not breaking new ground. It may be helpful to talk a little about the background and context of this call, however, so that we can form a further understanding of its significance.

The Ascendancy of Spirituality

The PM's promotion of her faith, at the instant of her inauguration, in a sense symbolises the ascendancy of spirituality, which we are witnessing in Jamaica. By crediting God with her arrival at this position of responsibility and by seeking divine leading in the pursuit of future tasks, the PM is reaching beyond herself to fulfil the promises she has made and to meet the expectations of the masses. By hanging her address on a prayer, the PM is hoping for miracles, which is what happens when God is believed to intervene. Certainly, when one thinks of the situation with crime, violence and the attitude to human life, one has to pray and hope for a miracle! Scientists in the social, economic and political fields have not yet helped us, so seeking help from another trinity cannot be called unrealistic. Mind you, the PM, in reference to her faith in God, may soon come to be ridiculed by the many anti-religious, secularists, whose support for her was more 'anti-P.J.' and 'anti-doctorates' than anything else.

Interest in Spirituality

The ascendancy of spirituality, of which I speak, however, is not to be confused with interest in going to church or church membership. In fact, statistics indicate that interest in spirituality has held firm or is increasing but, with the exception of one or two cases, church membership is declining. The spirituality in question, then, is the expressed wish to find a purpose for one's life that is more reliable than the secular, naturalistic, scientific definitions. The inability of these approaches to offer meaning and hope has led to a growing suspicion of them and has gone hand in hand with a questioning of their authority.

The court case in Kansas, USA, last year, in which it was argued that the theory of evolution was simply a theory to be taught alongside other theories, illustrates that questioning. Recalling Anselm's arguments for the existence of God, the proponents of the theory of Intelligent Design (ID) hold that the existence of the universe and of living things are best explained with reference to an intelligent cause. In their view, intelligent causality is a better idea than the 'undirected process such as natural selection,' which is a central claim of the evolutionary theory. In Christian terms, it is better to say, 'In the beginning, God.'

Fears

A brief perusal of recent stories in the print media can also illustrate the ascendancy of the spiritual. I must confess though that I do have some trepidation about this and hope our present political leadership does not come to confuse political interests with religious affections. History is replete with instances of the distortions of both faith and politics that occur when there is this confusion. The world cringed in horror when President Bush declared, in effect, that his decision to attack Iraq was directed by God. As outrageous as that decision, the war and the consequences are to us, there are many in the U.S.A. whose support for it is the belief that the man acted under the direction of the Holy Spirit, so it must be right. We have indications of those distortions rising now in our midst with so-called prophets claiming to have predicted the rise of Madam Portia to power.

The problem with claims of this nature is the difficulty there is to make a line of demarcation between the religious beliefs and the implied political wishes. To my mind there is nothing wrong with a religious leader expressing his political preferences. There is something questionable, however, when religious beliefs are harnessed to give credibility to political interests. By the same token, I hope that the religious affections of the PM will never be used to conceal her political motives.

A FEMALE PRIMATE TO THE RESCUE?
JULY 2, 2006

The election recently of Bishop Katherine Jefferts Schori, as the presiding bishop of the Episcopal Church in the United States, could be a mixed blessing for the Church, which seems to be heading for a major split. This interesting development for the Anglican Communion took place on June 20, 2006, during the church's 75th General Convention in Columbus Ohio. Although the female primate was elected by a small margin from a field of seven, six of whom were men, she is probably the best candidate for the job and who knows, maybe she has come to this primatial office for such a time as this. In this election, the Anglican Church in the United States positions itself years ahead of provinces like those in the Caribbean, United Kingdom and Ireland, where the election of a female primate will not happen for another 100 years. Such a period of time is also likely to elapse before provinces in Africa even begin to consider the idea of a female bishop much less to elect one.

The female ascent to primacy in the U.S. Episcopal Church comes as no real surprise but is in reality a logical development from the election of its first female bishop. In 1989, the Church created history when it elected Barbara Harris, a black social activist, as bishop. One knew then that it would only be a matter of time, and for many a matter of justice and credible development, for the present scenario to come to pass. Since then, several other women have been elected to the office of bishop, Katherine herself was elected Bishop of Nevada in 2001.

Greater Significance

It could be argued that from the point of view of the tradition of the Church, the election of a female as bishop is of greater significance than the election of a primate. Like the positions of cardinal or pope in the Roman Catholic Church, the position of primate is not an order of ministry, the orders being deacon, priest (or presbyter) and bishop. The difference, of course, is that the primate in the Anglican communion does not have the kind of authority that we associate with the cardinal, which is the corresponding position in the Roman Catholic Church. A major theological battle was won for women in 1989, then, when it was demonstrated in the election of Bishop Barbara, that none of the three orders of ministry are exclusive to men.

Interpreting Tradition

The election of Bishop Katherine as primate reinforces the principle of the inclusion of women at all levels of decision making in the Episcopal church but it could also accelerate the race towards a split because of the way in which Bishop Katherine seems to interpret tradition and development in the Church. Her detractors have pointed to the fact that coming as she has from formation in the field of science, her election already represents a break with the tradition in which there was a long, slow rise through years of theological formation and experience to leadership in the Church.

Threat to Unity

The threat to unity that her election represents, though, is that she is one of those bishops who voted in favour of the election of the declared homosexual, Gene Robinson, as Bishop of New Hampshire. That decision by the American Episcopalians landed the whole Anglican Communion into disarray because most of the other provinces of the communion cannot find the clear, unequivocal basis in the tradition of the church or scripture to justify allowing known homosexuals into the ordained ministry, much less to ordain them as bishop. It is here that the new primate will have her work cut out among her peers. She will have the task of demonstrating the credibility of this development in the life of the church.

However, even before she gets to the next Lambeth Conference, where bishops of the Anglican Communion gather every four years, she will face the challenge of convincing a large section of her church in the U.S. to remain united and to accept her leadership not so much because of her sex, but more so because of her position on homosexuality. The problem that Bishop Katherine faces in justifying the development, in which homosexuality is treated as normal, is one that is fundamental to how we understand the development of doctrine and practice in the Church. This is not a new problem.

Corrupted Development

A little over 100 years ago, this very issue of how doctrine develops was engaging the Church and led Henry Newman, who converted to Catholicism from the Anglican church, to write the book, An Essay on the Development of Christian Doctrine, 1898. Newman's book made headlines in church circles about the same time that Darwin's did. Darwin's epoch making publication, The Origin of Species by Natural Selection, was making the headlines all around. Newman's objective was to provide a basis on which to judge which doctrinal developments were credible and which were corruption. That undertaking by Newman was occasioned by the critique that Protestants were making of practices in the Roman Catholic doctrines, for example the veneration of the Virgin Mary, for which the justification could not be found in scripture. Space does not allow us here to go into the details of Newman's seven bases (preservation of type, continuity of principles, assimilation, logical sequence, anticipation of its developments, conservative action, and chronic vigour).

However, what is clear is that the development that favours the growing acceptance of the practice of homosexuality is a radical departure from tradition and cannot be explained with reference to any of Newman's widely accepted bases. Bishop Katherine, then, may have to account for this development with reference to Darwin's theory of natural selection. It is probably the case that the secular, pagan and plural context of today's world is one in which a 'corrupted development' is best adapted to survive.

DR. LEWIN WILLIAMS AND CARIBBEAN THEOLOGY, OCTOBER 1, 2006

In the recent death of Rev. Dr. Lewin Williams, President of the United Theological College of the West Indies (UTC), the Caribbean church community has lost a very gracious and dedicated theologian. As with the death of those who are neither rich nor powerful, there is a temptation to quickly pass over the event, especially as we in Jamaica have become so accustomed to death and dying. In 1994, Peter Lang Publishing Company released what has become Dr. William's opus magnum, under the title Caribbean Theology. The publication is significant because it is probably the most comprehensive Caribbean theological reflection we have received in the last decade.

It was not always the case that the realities of the Caribbean featured in the way that people in the region reflected on their faith. In fact, it is quite the case still today that churches and religious communities rely on what is happening abroad, especially in America, to dictate the character and content of their Christian life and action. There are three main movements that influenced the rise of Caribbean theology. The first was the struggle for political independence, which came to fruition in the region in the 1960s. Therefore, Caribbean theology represents an attempt to formulate a theological discourse that would complement the political imaginations of regional independence. Consequently, there is in Caribbean theology, a major emphasis on the idea of the decolonisation of theology. The central thought is that the church must also disassociate itself from colonial theology (European/American) if it is to contribute to the social reconstruction in the region. The missionary thrust in the Caribbean was, in many respects, a movement of cultural imposition. According to Watty, also a former president at United Theological College, those missionary activities could be termed 'imperialism at prayer' because in the mind of the missionaries, there was not always a clear distinction between evangelisation and Europeanisation.

Another movement that influenced the rise of Caribbean theology was the discourse on liberation theology that developed in Latin America. It emphasised social analysis of the actual conditions in which oppressed people were living, reading and questioning the Bible in light of the situations of oppression and taking action to change the situation of the oppressed. The third influence is the Black Power movement, which swept across the Americas, reaching the height of its glory during the 1960s. Of course, one of the earliest inspirations of the movement was Marcus Garvey, who disseminated a unique brand of African nationalism and black pride through the Universal Negro Improvement Association (UNIA) that he organised in 1914. The Caribbean theological discourse draws on the ideals of the Black Power movement in stressing the need for the indigenisation of faith and racial consciousness.

Williams and Indigenisation

The thesis of his book is that the rise of an indigenous Caribbean theological discourse is a backlash to European missionary activity, which went hand in hand with European geo-political expansion. He illustrates this marriage between colonialism and European evangelisation with reference to an incident in Guyana. He quotes an English Anglican clergyman who said: "We owe it to the negro to think for him, to help him by placing over him trustworthy men, armed with almost feudal authority to enforce such social duties as devolve upon him, and to save him from himself." [p. 5].

This kind of presumptuousness in the thinking of our Christian forbears, Dr. Williams argued, was detrimental to the Caribbean region. The development of a process in Caribbean theological thought, which emphasised cultural and racial respect, was a necessary corrective to the European missionary ideal. According to Dr. Williams, the failure of Caribbean thinkers to see this as an authentic enterprise suggests that there may be some lingering need for European blessing on the process. The failure to develop a truly indigenous church and the failure to expand indigenous Caribbean theological thought are probably the main reasons that Christian ideals are not seen to be making a significant impact on the character of life in the country.

We only have to look at the anomaly in which a myriad of churches populate the depressed communities, amidst extensively high levels of crime, violence and poverty, to see evidence of the failure. Part of the reasons churches are at a loss about how to deal with the realities of day to day life in Jamaica is that we continue to borrow the language and ideas for the way that we think and speak from foreign contexts. Pastors should pay greater attention to the surveys coming out of the social science faculty at UWI, the Survey of Living Conditions and the reports of the different task forces on crime and violence and read them alongside their bible.

In the long run, those reports are more critical to Sunday-morning preaching than the fuzzy ideas about people being afflicted with spirits and the need to convert Muslims, which we see coming out of America. Focusing on the realities of Jamaica and putting transformation in real and visible terms at the centre of our thinking is what Dr. Williams means by indigenisation in Caribbean theology. The enduring contribution of Dr. Lewin Williams, then, is that the relevance of the Caribbean church is always going to be judged by its commitment to social transformation, genuine independence and cultural respect.

A SIGNIFICANT CHURCH MILESTONE, MARCH 4, 2007

Had that event of March 1, 1457, not set precedence for Protestant Christianity, it could well have passed without notice. Yet, despite the many distractions, like World Cup fever, this important milestone in church history beckons us. The event of which we speak is the 550th anniversary of the establishment of the worldwide Moravian church. Calling attention to this anniversary is ironic because many people do not know that of which we speak. Yet, the demand of the moment is not so much for us to fill in the gaps in our memory and knowledge. Rather, a greater need is for churches in Jamaica to look at themselves, something which overconfidence or lack of beauty normally prevent us from doing. For this and other reasons, the Moravian Church has not planned celebrations to mark the occasion. Instead, this should be seen as a moment before the mirror, a moment to look, a sort of introspection.

The first reality that greets us on closer observation is that the Moravian Church is the oldest Protestant church it is quite small and relatively unknown. With a worldwide membership of just about one million adherents, it is the smallest of the worldwide communions. The reason for this irony lies in the fact that despite its claimed and demonstrated zeal for the missionary activities, that zeal was never translated into strategies for growing the denomination. The history of the church is replete with instances in which

Moravian missionaries initiated work and then handed it over to others to grow. From the point of view of the theology of missions, the Moravian Church is known more for planting than for nurturing. The feature of the Moravian Church as "a little old church" can probably be balanced by the fact that it has had a clearly articulated vision of its role in society. The clarity of the Church's vision and mission has not only contributed to longevity but has also ensured that the contributions it has made locally and globally go well beyond what one might expect of such a small religious community. In other words, "it likkle but it tallawah" (i.e it is small but powerful).

The Shift to Africa

The second thing to be seen is that although the Church was established as a European Church, the centre of gravity and growth of the communion has shifted to Africa. This is true for all the world communions. The largest provinces, the largest number of new ventures and the centres of real numerical growth are all located in Africa. The Moravian Church in Jamaica has responded to this shift by recruiting missionaries from the beloved continent for work in Jamaica. The shift of the centre to Africa has not only opened up the opportunities for South-South cooperation but also evidenced a return of compliment by Africa, which received missionaries from Jamaica in the 19th century. It is only a pity that the church, and others churches with a European heritage, has been so slow to lay aside the European weight and influence that have so afflicted its life, liturgy and worship. The sooner we do this the better it will be for the denomination.

The third thing we see in this 550th anniversary of the worldwide Moravian Church is probably the most difficult to digest. The church has maintained a reputable ecumenical character and has stressed unity as part of its self-understanding. However when the church was establishment in 1457, that initiative created a precedence of division, from which Protestant Christianity has not recovered. Sadly, it is the fountainhead of the ever-increasing formation of new churches. The readiness with which leaders start churches they call their own, and the perpetual struggle for power have become unfortunate blots that undermine Christian witness. Looking at the plurality of churches in Jamaica, for example, it is safe to argue that the propensity to divide is part and parcel of Protestantism. The diversity and "one-up-manship", which leaders of Protestant Christianity so cherish is a weakness and a major stumbling block in the effort to engender wholeness, unity and reform in the nation's life.

The Roman Catholic and Orthodox churches tending to defend the political and social status quo, are much more effective in bringing about social change because of the internal unity and clear lines of authority that characterise them. Nevertheless, the churches should consider whether we are not part of the problem in Jamaica. It is a sobering observation for the Christian community that the rapid social deterioration and spiralling in violence and crime in Jamaica occurred at the same moment when there was a sharp increase in the numbers of churches. Recovering the unity imperative within a religiously diverse Jamaican society is a challenge that recounting the founding of the Moravian Church 550 years ago brings.

Radicalism and Reform

The final thing we see in our reflective observation is that although the Moravian Church arose out of a tradition of radicalism and reform, it has tended to portray itself as conservative and pacific. The establishment of the Moravian Church 550 years ago was possible because the Hussite Movement, which was a socio-political movement, succeeded. The ideals of that movement were: (1) freedom of preaching; (2) communion in both kinds; (3) poverty of the clergy and expropriation of church property; (4) punishment of notorious sinners. On the face of it these ideals, called the Four Articles of Prague, were also religious ideals but one could not miss their social and political implications. These articles feature significant in the Bohemian war that their promulgation set in motion.

The problem with the way many churches state their ideals today is that these ideals cannot be translated into concrete actions that will affect communal life on a day to day basis. The minimising of the reforming and radical tradition was a succumbing to the pressures of some of the newer churches, which were experiencing numerical growth. As Ashley Smith once said, churches resort to the use of certain defensive measures, out of fear of losing themselves [Real Roots and Potted Plants]. This could be the reason that churches in Jamaica seem to be more at home in the heavens than on the earth. However, if the mission of the church does not remain on the ground, our impact on national life will be minimal. For 1457 to be worthy of mention in 2007, it is imperative that the heritage of radicalism and reform is recovered.

RELIGIONS AND ECONOMIC SUCCESS, JUNE 2014

In a 2012 survey by the Washington-based PEW Research centre, it was established that 84% (5.8b) of the world's population claimed affiliation with one of the religious traditions of the world. The implication of this is that religious theories and religious cultures are pervasive. It strikes me then as being ironic that religions have been pushed or is being pushed to the periphery of public discourse by those who control public media. Given the pervasive nature of religions and religious theories, in this article I will make the assertion that it is reasonable to consider them at the centre of public discourse, not least in relation to discussion about economic success.

Despite the fact that many affluent societies have relatively high percentages of religious affiliation, for example USA 78%, UK 70%, Luxembourg 70%, Finland 80%, one cannot claim a direct cause-effect relationship between religious affiliation and affluence. In fact, some will argue that the converse is true because some of the poorest countries in the world have high levels of religious affiliation, for example Ethiopia 96% Haiti 87%, Niger 98%. Lest anyone might rush to a conclusion here, it is to be noted that two countries not known for their affluence, namely, North Korea and Czeck Republic, have the highest percentage of non-religious (71% and 76% respectively). So there is no necessary direct correlation between poverty and religious affiliation and religion is not simply a habit of the poor. The pervasive nature of religious affection and, at the same time, the uncertainty of the role that religion might play in society's fortune, make it reasonable to raise the question about the possible role that religions might play in economic fortunes.

Taking Religions Seriously

In the aforementioned survey by the PEW Research centre, the world's 6.9 billion people are divided into two major cultural blocks: the religious and the non-religious. The assumption governing this division of the human community is that one either claims to have a religious affiliation and or one does not. One can indeed take objection to the theoretical assumption but, if it is allowed, then everyone falls into one of these two major cultures. I say culture because of the worldviews that exist in these two groups. For example, one group takes religions seriously and makes allowance for religious values and ideas to influence day to day activity and decisions. In the other group, religions tend not to be given any credence and will not feature in either day to day activity or decisions.

However, it is the 84% religious affiliation, in particular, that prompts the assertion that one should take religions and religious cultures seriously. Further sub-culture categorisation show Christians at 31%, Muslims at 23%, Hindu at 15% etc. By this cultural categorisation, the third largest block is of those having no religious affiliation at 16%. The question then is how is it that a religious worldview is having lesser and lesser role is the determination of public discourse? How is it that there is no consideration of religious factors in economic success?

The variety and diversity in the religious tradition is part of the reason they should be overlooked. If religious cultures are lacking in their power or capacity to influence public discourse, it is probably due to their conflicting claims and the diversity of their opinions. Take for example the situation in

Christianity. Each centre of authority, for example a worldwide communion or denomination, can be further subdivided in several mini-centres of authority and beliefs. This amazing variety is religious claims and sub-cultures and how to reckon with competing claims among them, is what led to my major publication, A Protestant Theology of Religious Pluralism, 2009. It aimed to find a theological discourse that can overcome the clash of claims from within the Protestant sub-cultures. The point to be noted though is the diversity is part of what ensures the pervasive nature of religions and helps to account for the 84% affiliation worldwide.

The alarming diversity is also evident in Islam. This fact seems to be forgotten by many who associate Islam with negative caricatures that are frequently thrown up in the public media. The variety must, therefore, caution us in the way we speak of the Islamic faith. My own effort to find language to help guide conversation between Christian and Islamic cultures led to the publication of A Formula for Conversation: Christians and Muslims in Dialogue, 2007.

Economic Failure

Despite the fact that theorist are not inclined to reckon with religions in economic matters, neither the theories of religious "irrationality" nor those of economic "rationality" have been able to solve the problem of human deprivation and inequality. The extent of world inequality and deprivation can be illustrated with reference to the Global Wealth Pyramid. Take, for example, the fact that 69% of the world's population lives on less than €140 per week, which is less than what the Irish Government gives for social welfare payment. For this reason, at the very least, one should consider what might be lacking in conventional theories of economic success.

Following the PEW research categorisation, it can be said that theories about successful human living can also be divided into two sets, one religious and the other non-religious. On the religious side we have, for example, the Christian, the Islamic, the Hindu and the Buddhist. They reflect claims and aspirations of 76% of the world's population. One should not under estimate, for example, the impact that the Buddhist commitment to the 7-fold paths to Nirvana, or the Hindu desire to avoid reincarnation at a lower level of being, or the Muslim belief in the way of the Qur'an, or the Christian belief in the way of Jesus, will have on how economic success is construed.

On the non-religious side there are the economic theories, for example of Adam Smith (1723-1790), Karl Marx (1818-1883), John Maynard Keynes (1883-1946), Friedrich Hayek (1899-1992) and Milton Friedman (1912-2006). They have been classed as the five apostles of economic theories. There are other contemporary theorists, who are classed as Neo-Classical, Endogenous, Cumulative or the New Economic Geography. Their viewpoints are based on combinations of aspects of the views of the five apostles. They have different emphases about the role of the individual in the free market and the roles of government and government policy. The variety of emphases should not surprise us because the determinants of economic dynamism do not have the same influence in all countries and sub-cultures alike. What leads to success in one country will not necessarily lead to success in another. In other words, economic theories are not sure to succeed in bringing about wealth and success in economies. In fact, the inequality that has persisted in the world gives the indication that the economic theories have not really succeeded. The differences in the religious theories and how they might contribute to economic success is the issue to which we now turn.

Spiritual Capital and Economics

The contribution that the religious theories can and do make to economic activity is in the area of spiritual capital. Probably the best definition of what constitutes spiritual capital is from Chris Baker and Hannah Skinner, who in their research funded by the William Temple Foundation, defined Spiritual as the values, ethics, beliefs and vision which faith communities bring to civil society at the global and local level. It also refers to the holistic vision for change held within an individual's set of beliefs. Spiritual capital in this form can be described as more liquid than solid because it relates to intangibles such as ideas and visions and is not exclusively claimed by a specific religious tradition.

Spiritual Capital is not a recent invention but has been around since Adam Smith's Wealth of Nations, 1776. The idea arose in the writings of Adam Muller, as part of his critique of Adam Smith's failure to ascribe a greater role to religious culture and theory. Therefore, When Max Weber began writing The Protestant Work Ethic and the Spirit of Capitalism in the 1920's, he was seeking to making application of what Adam Muller a century before called spiritual capital.

Each religious tradition has core teachings and values, which have a critical bearing on economic prudence and economic success. The Judeo-Christian proverb, that a false balance is an abomination underpins the imperative for fairness with respect to standards for goods in earlier economies. The concept of quality assurance and quality checks, in modern economies, arise from the same. The Qur'anic teaching on the wrongful acquisition of property has implications today not only for appropriate payment for land but also for oil and mineral. It is not without significance that the structure of inequality between in the nations is related to payments for minerals and oil. The Hindu concept of Karma, which is based on the law of consequence, if observed, would have been a hedge against the recent deterioration in the in the world financial system, in which actors had little regard to consequence and bad karma. Finally, at the centre of the Buddhist 8th Fold steps to Nirvana stands the concept of perfect livelihood. For the Buddhist, a livelihood that is built, for example in the arms trade, is ethically suspect. Consider the difference it would make if resources used for arms were to be invested in a sustainable economy.

Conclusion

Religious theories and economic theories aspire to provide strategies to secure the well-being, wealth and sustainability of the countries of the world. Yet these countries have developed in unequal and inconsistent ways. Given the economic failures at the world level, and the persistence of inequality and deprivation, economists can hardly gloat about the success of their theories in bringing wealth to the nations. Harnessing and deploying the spiritual capital of the religious traditions might be a way to breathe fresh life into attempts for economic success.

Chapter Four

Letters to the Editor

COMMENTS ON RELIGIOUS ARTICLES, DECEMBER 21, 1990

The Editor, Sir

I write to comment on the article "An Upsurge in Religion" In the Gleaner 1990 Annual. The writer, Mr Billy Hall, refers to articles by Ian Boyne and Conrad Lindo respectively as the "Dabler's collection" and "lacking serious research." Having read both writers many times during the year and I would agree with that description only to a small extent. I suspect that Mr Hall did not share their opinions on many occasions, judging from responses he himself wrote. What is more significant, however is that Mr Hall in his article seems to be guilty of the same sin with which he charges Mr Lindo. If it is that Mr Hall's article was attempting to give an over-view of the situation in the religious life of the country, then it surprises me that no real mention is made of other religions apart from Christianity.

But that aside, I am even more surprised at how superficially Mr. Hall has gleaned. For instance, all the persons he seemed to have interviewed are in the Corporate Area. The reality of religious life, but more specifically church life in South-Western Jamaica, is other than described in "An Upsurge in Religion. "Changes in church attendance and membership, as well as financial intake, do not support that view. In fact, a more careful research by the writer would have revealed that, for many such churches, there is (a) disillusionment as the faithful struggle to come to terms with the economic realities, (b) despair, because churches have failed to hold out for members any real hope of changes in their situation, socially and otherwise, and (c) decline, due in part to heavy migration to the corporate area and overseas In short, the failure of the churches to respond creatively to the day to day needs of the faithful have led to attrition, not upsurge. The failure to do careful research has led Mr Hall to gloss over the differences in church life between rural and urban Jamaica.

I am. etc
Livingstone Thompson
Springfield P O, St. Elizabeth

EARLY ROLE OF THE MORAVIANS, JANUARY 17, 1991

The Editor, Sir:

On December 9, 1754, while the Roman Catholic Church and the Church of England (Anglican) focused their ministry entirely on the planter class. In the then slave society, a small group of Christians, from a denomination originating in Europe, landed in Jamaica. (This was before the Baptists, Methodists, or Presbyterians) Though they had to get approval from the planters, their work was exclusively with the slaves. For more than half a century this denomination did not put up a permanent structure for worship. This was due partly to the fact that the missionaries were not from a denomination with a "cathedral" tradition, but also to the fact that resources for such construction among the slaves were very limited.

However, 1816, 52 years later, the first church building was put up. In 1979 when this denomination celebrated its 225th anniversary in Jamaica, the stones of this first building were used to put up a monument at Bogue in St. Elizabeth. This was quite significant, because the denomination is known more for its monuments than for its cathedrals. One such monument is the first elementary school to be established in Jamaica. This was built at Rowe's Corner, near Alligator Pond in 1823. The present Lititz All-Age School, in St. Elizabeth, is a relocation of this first elementary school. But there are several "cathedrals" of which the denomination may speak. The church buildings at Mispah in Walderstan, Manchester, at Bethabara in Newport, Manchester, at Carmel in Westmoreland and Springfield and Lititz in St. Elizabeth range from 100 to 150 years old. The denomination I speak of is the Moravian Church. I consider it necessary to inform you of this as the writer of the article on "Established Churches" in the Sunday Magazine of January 6, 1991 seemed unaware of it. The article made no mention of the Moravian Church pictorially or otherwise. It is hard to tell whether this is oversight or sheer ignorance.

I am, etc
Rev. Livingstone Thompson

A COMMENT ON C. REYNOLDS' PLEA FOR "SENSE," NOVEMBER 12, 1998

I always enjoy reading C. Roy Reynolds. Frankly, I think he is one of the most engaging writers in the print media today. His article in The Gleaner on Tuesday, November 10, 1998 entitled "Let's Talk Sense, please!" was another example. He forced me to read all the way to the end. This article may be regarded as a partial response to one of the issues he raised. Though I do not know him personally, I should not find it hard to make him out in the crowd. He is likely to be one of those persons talking to himself, because I'm sure he likes to speak to a sensible person. Let me caution him, however, about learning to listen to others. Even the dull and ignorant have their story. Mr. Reynolds suggests that the idea of thanking God for hearing our prayers, in the passing of Hurricane Mitch, is "illogical." This conclusion he seems to arrive at because we are unable to explain why Jamaica was spared and Central America was not. He seems to understand such thanksgiving as a suggestion that the people of Jamaica are "more moral" people. If we forgive his use of the expression "more moral" for the time being, let's see if we can make sense of the rest.

There are two different facts in the events. One is that Jamaica was spared and the other that Central America was not. Taking the first, the question then becomes what might be our response to the fact that we were spared. To my mind, we have three options. First, we could regret it and are sorrowful, thinking as some do, that we deserve the disaster. That response would be deserving of the charge of being sadistic. Secondly, we could disregard it, treating it as an accident or a coincidence of nature. Such is the response of people who see nature and its laws as the highest authority, to which they can appeal. In this kind of thinking, there is a natural explanation for everything under the sun. This, presumably, is the position of Mr. Reynolds. If that is the case, then I invite him or anyone that holds this view of life, to give the natural explanation of why life commenced in the universe. Why is there a universe?

Why do human beings have the capacities to show kindness even to those who mean them harm? Why do we grow old? There is a third possible response however, to the fact that Jamaica was spared the hurricane. It is that we may rejoice. I should hope that rejoicing is not illogical! The sensible man in Reynolds' description seems to have the capacity to rejoice, if even at his wisdom. I chose to give thanks to God for sparing us because I accept that God is final authority. But that thanksgiving is not one filled with triumphalism or any suggestion that it had anything to do with me. On the contrary, it recognises that it had nothing to do with me. God's will is not a reward for my prayers. My prayer was that in a certain event, (Jamaica being spared), God would be glorified and praised. It is a much more challenging action to praise God notwithstanding the ravages of the disaster. When nature is your god, that may not be difficult. Those who want to give thanks to nature for sparing us make nature their god. Everyone should be allowed to thank his or her god. Therefore, our response to the fact that Jamaica was spared depends upon our understanding of life and existence. It is about who we conceive God to be and the way in which we understand God to be involved in human affairs. I think rather than "cursing" people for crediting God with their salvation, Reynolds should go ahead and give the logical explanations that need not result in praise to God.

Inequalities

The fact that Central America was not spared the onslaught of 'Mitch,' as is the case with any natural disaster, does pose a challenge to faith in God. For the persons who see nature as the final authority, they have no problem with natural disasters. For them, the poor people there were just unfortunate. I am sorry that I do not have an easier answer as to why some people suffer so much the ravages of disaster. What I do know is that the suffering of the poor and the vulnerable exposes the inequalities in the world. The moment of the suffering of our neighbours will certainly test our willingness to be good neighbours, knowing that they are not any more deserving of the disaster than we are. Will our response remain that of the "natural person" who counts them as unfortunate? Or will we have the insight to see that in their suffering, they bear the consequences of what it means to live in our world, a world of sin! This does not mean they are being punished. It means that they are suffering even though they are no more deserving than others are. In that sense, their suffering is vicarious. The matter of human suffering, especially as a result of natural disasters, is far too profound an issue to respond to by saying they are simply unfortunate. Reynolds is of the view that "one of the great deficiencies of religion is the way it tends to get in the way of human conscience. This, I suggest, is not a deficiency of religion as much as it is a deficiency of ideology.

People who practise the same religion draw different consequences from its maxims. When many that called themselves Christians were supporting apartheid, others who claimed allegiance to the same faith were denouncing it. Unfortunately, there are many issues in life that do not have easy solutions. There are many questions that do not have easy answers. Some think that to have faith in God provides easy answers to life's difficult questions. In my experience, faith in God is no guarantee for easy answers. On the contrary, because of faith in God, the answers are more difficult to come by, because they are never simply or natural. But then that is the nature of faith. Moreover, some people have faith in God, others just do not.

RE-INTERPRETING CHRISTIAN TRADITION AND HISTORY

The Editor,
Jamaica Daily Gleaner
Dear Editor,

A recent discussion on the Radio Jamaica News Programme "Beyond the Headlines" (June 11, 2003) has prompted me to raise for further consideration by the Christian community the following question: are there not several authentic ways of reading and interpreting the Christian faith? In the discussion, Dr. Lucien Jones, Mrs. Barbara Glouden (both Anglicans) and Fr. Ramkisoon, a Roman Catholic Priest, were responding to questions about homosexuality and its place in Christian ethics. The discussion was prompted by the ruling of a count in Canada allowing gay couples to be married. We in the Moravian Church regard homosexuality as a deviant sexual practice. However, Mrs. Glouden is right in suggesting that despite the fact that we might have very rigid views on the subject, that does not preclude the need for discussion. We might find that there are differing opinions among Christians in Jamaica even on this question.

My concern however is not with homosexuality per se. Rather, I would like to raise the broader issue of how we read the Bible and Christian tradition. Much of the way in which we understand what we read today in Christian history and the Holy Bible has been influenced by the tradition whose authority we accept. It is for this reason that the Seventh Day Adventist tradition represents a critique to the traditional Christian practice of observing Sunday as the main Christian day of worship. Anglicans question the Roman Catholic understanding of infallibility. Baptists question Anglicans and Moravians in their understanding of episcopacy and oversight. Churches in general do not allow ministers from other churches to preside at their Holy Communion services, even though they could be allowed to preach. The Roman Catholics cannot find biblical justification for admitting women to the priesthood, whereas the Anglicans can find no biblical justification for their exclusion. The Moravians, Methodists, Orthodox Churches and others subscribe to the practice of infant baptism on the basis of its authenticity within the longest Christian tradition, whereas the Baptists and a whole lot of other churches see no authentic Christian tradition to support that practice. Protestants in general observe only two sacraments whereas Anglicans, Roman Catholics and Orthodox say there are seven sacraments. More critically, some churches insist that speaking in unknown tongues is the only real evidence that the Holy Spirit has baptised a person but others question the reading of the Bible on which this position is based. Notwithstanding these differences, however, the churches all claim to be standing in the authentic Christian tradition. Who is to adjudicate between these different claims?

It seems that Christians need to admit two truths about their faith: (1) We are inclined to accept the reading of the Bible and Christian history that is given by someone whose authority we accept. For some people this means they will accept only what they themselves read and choose to believe. (2) There are different ways of reading and interpreting Christian doctrines and Christian history. There is no position that is free from biases.

The issue then to be addressed in Christian discourse is how to dialogue given the fact that we are all biased in favour of our own approach, which we believe to be the most authentic. Mrs Glouden is right. We cannot side-step the issue of dialogue. Even so, some people are quite prepared to live in the illusion that the way they understand the Christian tradition is the only correct way.

I am
Livingstone Thompson
Moravian Church Office
3 Hector Street, Kingston 5

MORAVIAN POSITION ON HOMOSEXUALITY, NOVEMBER 2, 2003

The Editor, Sir:

Recently, a number of articles have appeared in The Gleaner dealing with the issue of homosexuality. For the benefit of your readers I want to share the statement that was adopted by the Moravian Church in 1995. This statement represents the position of the Moravian Church on the issue at this time. In the understanding of the Moravian Church, marriage between a man and a woman forms the ideal framework for intimate sexual relationship between two persons. It is therefore the duty and privilege of all members to uphold the ideals of Christian marriage, and to avoid anything that would bring dishonour upon it.

The church, nevertheless, recognises and affirms the choice of persons to remain single. This is in no way a dishonouring of the ideals of Christian marriage. The church continues to affirm, consistent with scripture, that marriage, that is to say, the formal, public and legal union between a man and a woman is the only relationship in which sexual intercourse may be practised. The church is therefore opposed to any practice which conflicts with this ideal.

The 1982 Synod of the Moravian Church in Jamaica adopted the following resolution: Be it resolved that this synod condemns the evil practice of homosexuality and recommends that a consultative body comprising the church and Government be set up to provide counselling and advice in eliminating this evil from the society. Be it resolved that the granting of licences to operate gay clubs be abandoned. The 1995 Synod of the church remains firm in its opposition to the practice even though it continues in the society. Persons who believe in and practice homosexuality are regarded as having deviant tendencies and must be treated as being in need of help and counselling. The church takes a caring rather than a condemning attitude to such persons and opposes any form of violence against them.

The church is opposed to any effort to make the practice of homosexuality legal, as this is contrary to our understanding of scripture and of God's intention for human sexual relations.

I am etc.,
Livingstone Thompson (Rev Dr.)
President The Moravian Church in Jamaica

GANJA CASE NOT STRONG ENOUGH, DECEMBER 27, 2003

The Editor, Sir:

I was hoping that I would have found in the Report of the National Commission on Ganja, 2001, a serious and well-argued case to support the well-known and popular view that the use of ganja in small quantities should be decriminalised. However, after reading the Report, I have to conclude that the Commission, notwithstanding the hard work put into the project, missed a critical opportunity to lay the question to rest once and for all.

The Report, unfortunately, suffers from a number of defects. This, I believe, was due to the fact that the Commission was overwhelmed: "the overwhelming majority of persons appearing before the Commission feel that ganja should be decriminalised." (p. 16) The Commission seemed to have forgotten that the case had to be made, since the issue was a matter of changing the law. If the lawmakers were themselves sufficiently convinced that the law should be changed, they would have already brought the recommendation to the Parliament. The question at stake, then, is whether the Report makes the case.

Defects

The first defect that the Report suffers from is that nowhere in the report is the actual text of the law relating to the use of ganja quoted, although we are told that it relates to "Sections 7C and 7D" of the Dangerous Drugs Act. The Report therefore proceeds on the assumption that everyone knows what the law says. This may seem to be a simple matter but if a case is being made for a certain provision to be changed, then do we not need to know exactly what the provisions states? I have never seen the text of the law that relates to the possession and use of ganja but I know what the reaction of the police is to possession and use. Given that the police sometimes act outside of the provisions of the law, it would be helpful if we saw in black and white the text we want to rescind.

The second defect of the Report is that it did not help the reader, by giving a historical account of what may have led to ganja use and possession being made a criminal offence. We are left to speculate about those reasons, which presumably are no longer relevant. What we are told is that, "up until the early years of the 20th century it [ganja] was widely used as a folk medicine and did not appear to constitute a major social problem." However, apart from the fact that we are living in a different historical period, which has the benefit of further scientific research, I do not know from this Report why the use and possession became a criminal offence.

Scientific Evidence

The third defect in the Report is that it does not offer any serious critique of the scientific evidence presented. The terms of reference required that the Commission "evaluate research and studies." However, Chapter 2, which deals with the Medical Science Literature, does not show evidence of critique. Rather, what we see is a cataloguing of the different opinions, some of which appear contradictory. For example in dealing with the effects of cannabis the Report states that, "intoxication with cannabis leads to slight impairment of psychomotor and cognitive function." (p.9) However, at another place in the same section the Report states that, "several studies have shown that cannabis is known to impair psychomotor performance in a wide variety of tasks." (p. 10) The difference may be simply the word "slight" but in science, "slight impairment" is different 'from "impairment."

Similarly, The Report states that it is felt that, "cannabis use is a weakly addictive drug but does induce dependence in a significant minority." (p.11) However, it goes on to quote Anthony and Helzer in asserting that, it is estimated that about half of those who use cannabis daily will become dependent." (p.11) Without any assessment of these two positions, we are left in the silence of the report to take a "significant minority" to mean fifty per cent. The absence of critique leaves the reader at the mercy of Zimmer and Morgan, who the Report quotes several times (in two and a half pages) in the section dealing with the effects on the brain. I feel as if 1 am being brainwashed - no pun intended!

Why Juveniles?

The fourth defect I see in the Report is that it does not explain why juveniles should not be allowed to use ganja where adults could be allowed. If it is good for medicine; if, as the Report in relying on Zimmer and Morgan claims that marijuana use "makes no significant contribution to high school students academic performance," (p. 12), then what is the problem with juveniles using it? What is rather ironic is that the Report seems to want it to remain a criminal offence for juveniles to use ganja in small quantities but not adults. I cannot understand this reasoning.

The Report claims that it would be "remarkable indeed, if the Commission did not receive depositions from the Rastafari community." (p.29). However, by juxtaposing the constitutional issue relating to the use of ganja in religion with recreational use, the Report has further complicated the issue. I call this a complication because it would seem that we are now dealing with the right of individuals to freely practice their religious faith, which right is protected by the constitution. It would seem from the prohibition that the denial of the free use of ganja in religious ceremonies is an infringement of a fundamental right. How is it then, that the Report does not raise that more important constitutional issue?

Religious Rites

Presumably the use of ganja as part of a religious rite by the Rastafarians preceded the law against marijuana use. Or is it the other way around? It would be helpful if the chronology were given here because it may well have shown that the Rastafarian argument for sacramental use was an attempt to circumvent what they perceived as an unjust law. In this regard the Report is not helpful. My problem, then, Editor, is that I was looking to the Report for help to make the case for decriminalisation. However, buoyed by the popular view that ganja should be decriminalised, the Commission simply reported that most people can't see the reason why its possession and use in small quantities should be a criminal offence. Let's say we now know what we suspected, that that view was widespread. Then, as Mrs. Beverly Anderson-Manley loves to ask on the Breakfast Club so we must now ask, "So where do we go from here"? One thing that is sure, we shall be overwhelmed as usual with ganja smoke this Christmas, whether we like it or not!

I am, etc.,
Livingstone Thompson, PhD
President of the Executive Board
Moravian Church in Jamaica

WHY THE JLP IS WARY OF THE SOCIAL PARTNERSHIP, JANUARY 23, 2004

The Jamaica Labour Party (JLP) seems suspicious of the Irish model of social partnership, in which the government, the private sector and the trade union have some growing common understanding. This emerging impasse reveals a fundamental difference between the politics on which the Irish model is predicated and Jamaican politics. The Irish model of social partnership is consistent with the electoral system of proportional representation, in which there is the expectation that there will be several players representing different parties that are elected in a given constituency. For example, when voters go to the poll, they do not usually vote for one candidate. They can, in principle vote for all the candidates in order of priority. So there will be a first choice, a second choice, a third choice and so on, irrespective of the party they represent. When the first choice candidate gets the requisite number of votes for election on the first count, any additional vote for that candidate is shared between the remaining candidates on a percentage basis, depending on how many votes they polled in the first count. Similarly, on the second count, once a candidate gets the requisite numbers of votes for election, their additional votes are shared with the rest of candidates on a similar percentage basis.

Representatives

The net effect of this is that one constituency can have several persons as representatives in the parliament. There is, then, a presumption of partnership in the way they practice their politics. In recent years, there has developed a tradition of coalition government in Ireland. The impression I got is that no one party wishes to be in government. The last election was a case in point. The Fine Fail Party could have pressed home the advantage that they had and seek election as a majority to govern on their own. However, in the campaign, they encouraged support for their coalition partner, the Progressive Democrats, even though there are several ways in which they differ on economic and social policies.

What is missing from our local politics is that presumption of partnership. The first past the post system that we use predisposes us to competition not partnership. This is the politics behind the suspicion of the Opposition.

I am, etc,
Livingstone Thompson

THE MURDER OF REV DR RWM CUTHBERT, FEBRUARY 29, 2004

The Editor, Sir:

February 24, 2004, is 19 years since the death of Rev. Dr. R.M. Cuthbert (1935-1985), former president of the Executive Board of Moravian Church. Dr. Cuthbert was shot and killed by unknown assailants as he drove along South Avenue but until now no one has been punished for that crime.

Calling attention to Cuthbert's death is relevant not only because he was killed a stone's throw from the place where Senior Superintendent Lloyd McDonald was shot and killed. It is also relevant because it reflects a pattern of brutality we have become used to seeing. We were reminded that SSP McDonald is the third security officer to be killed since the start of the year. In a, similar vein, when Cuthbert was killed in 1985, he was the third clergyman to be killed by gunmen in a fortnight. The Gleaner editorial on the Sunday following Cuthbert's murder said, "We hope the perpetrators of this particular murder will soon be brought to book." What we fear about the Superintendent's murder is that it will go the same way as Cuthbert's murder; no one will be brought to justice.

Until people who murder are made to pay and know that they will have to pay for the death of others, the mayhem is likely to continue. It seems that the credibility of the security forces hangs significantly on its ability to bring perpetrators of crime, especially crimes of this character, to justice. The police cannot afford to fail to bring the killers of their fellow officer to justice because it would reflect badly on their professional skills. It is a mockery to law and order if such daring crimes can be committed before witnesses and no one is made to pay.

So, my hope is that the killers for SSP McDonald will be found because only by punishing these criminals that we will reassure ourselves that we live in a society of law and order. Mind you, I have long given up hope that Cuthbert's killers will be found.

I am etc,
Livingstone Thompson

RECONSIDERING THE RIGHTS LAW, MARCH 3, 2006

The Editor, Sir:

I did not see Stephen Vasciannie's email address in his article today (Monday, February 27). I wanted to say to him that, as far as I know, the buggery law is still in force in Ireland and the U.K. and runs alongside the right to practise homosexuality. The whole issue is not so much whether homosexuality takes place in privacy, but whether it is between consenting adults. It seems to me that the buggery law in Jamaica, by the logic of the human rights argument, will become applicable only to cases where there is no consent.

Consenting Adults

Once the practice of homosexuality is predicated on the basis of human rights, there is no way one can then say that consenting adults may not have the freedom to do so. The problematic issue, at a more fundamental level, is how we understand human rights. The recent fiasco over the cartoon of the prophet Muhammad was, in effect, over the meaning of the right to free speech. We are on a slippery slope here, Stephen. The argument of the church leaders is related to an interpretation of human rights. Please, consider the issue more carefully.

I am, etc.,
Livingstone Thompson

Postscript

Jamaica's Programme of Advancement through Health and Education

Petal Thompson-Williams, M.Ed (UTech)

INTRODUCTION

Jamaica has traditionally relied on agriculture, bauxite and tourism as the main sources of income for economic growth and development. The country has however not been able to realise its potential for sustained growth and development. Instead the population has encountered severe poverty and the economy experiences low or no growth. According to Hassan, Idu, Uyo and Ogbole (2012), poverty is a foremost issue in the socio-political discourse of most third world countries. This view is relevant to Jamaica's socio-political situation and the government, in acknowledging this socio-economic need, has engineered policies and programmes to alleviate poverty and spur growth and development. Among the many policies to target welfare support to the poorest in the country is the PATH project. (Programme of Advancement Through Health and Education), which the Government of Jamaica introduced in 2002. The programme is one of the initiatives of the government designed to address the needs of the most vulnerable in the society. These include children from birth to the completion of secondary education; pregnant and lactating women and poor adults 18-59 years; the elderly 60 years or over and not in receipt of a pension and persons with disabilities. Beneficiaries of Health Grants are required to register in a Government Health Centre and maintain a prescribed schedule of visits. The schedule is determined by the beneficiary's age and benefit category. Children over 6 years of age must be attending a government funded school and must maintain a minimum monthly attendance record of 85%, in order to satisfy the conditionality for the education grant (Ministry of Labour and Social Security, 2006).

HEALTH

The issues of health and education are critical to a nation's growth development and sustainability. American poet Ralph Emerson says the first wealth is health. Appropriately so, healthcare is a PATH condition for state benefit; a healthy nation is a productive nation. Healthy persons will be more productive, alert and live longer while suffering fewer ailments in older age which will relieve the burden on the health system. Early and regular visits to Health Centres are a master move as it focuses on prevention. The old adage is therefore true, that an ounce of prevention is better than cure. The benefits of good health include but are not limited to the prevention of obesity, heart disease, diabetes and some forms of cancer. Most of the health problems listed above are associated with lifestyle choices. The need for early intervention in health, particularly for the most vulnerable, is due to the increase in life expectancy. In Jamaica the life expectancy for males is 71.8 and females 77.2. This is somewhat below the WHO average at 74.4 (WHO, 2013). What these numbers suggest is that if Jamaica is going to attain any kind of sustained development it must attend to good healthcare for its population from an early age.

EDUCATION

Education is the other key component for PATH beneficiaries. Education as a criterion provides the skills knowledge and competences needed for sustainable growth. The educated individual should be able to be critical thinkers, problem solvers and possess the necessary skills to survive in an ever changing world. It is these skills and competences that a nation will need to develop on a sustainable basis. PATH ensures access to all of the nation's people for equity and to widen the pool of professionals who will create viable employment or work to meet the nation's developmental goals. The educational level of a country is a determinant of the stage of its economic development and potential for future growth. Investment in education is important, enabling the development of each person's full potential and consequently creating a competitive workforce. Education is therefore a social indicator of a country's economic development and the stock and quality of its human capital (Vision 2030, Jamaica).

THE FUTURE

Since the inception of PATH, over 400,000 persons have benefitted (Gordon, 2013). The number will increase as the programme continues to expand and provide for those who are most in need. The project is necessary to ensure that all members of the population enjoy equity to health and education. However, if the beneficiaries of PATH do not see themselves as movers and changers, the end goal of sustainable development will not be achieved. There must be a relationship between PATH and the Jamaican economy for sustainable development.

One relationship which this document wishes to consider is the transition of PATH beneficiaries from dependency to independence as their social and economic status improve and there is a clear indication that investment in human capital has provided protection from economic risks. In order to achieve sustainable development economic growth must be achieved. Therefore, PATH beneficiaries in the working age group who have no limitations to be able to work should see the programme as a platform for independence and, as former beneficiaries, be inclined to a revolving system which will enable new beneficiaries. It is therefore the view of this writer that PATH should not be from the 'womb to the tomb.' Social welfare is a necessary policy of societies and there should be a culture engendered which provides assistance to reduce economic risk. The aim of social intervention should be to ensure that able bodied beneficiaries, upon graduation, will be able to work towards the achievement of training and skills to enable others to become beneficiaries. PATH should not be an incentive for persons not to seek to be gainfully employed. PATH should not be an incentive to have more children than one can afford. PATH isn't a reason or excuse not to prepare for retirement. Instead, PATH should encourage the productive spirit of the people so government will increase its income, the nation's productivity will increase and sustained development will become a reality.

The future is bright for Jamaica as more of its population has access to proper health care and prevention of diseases and illnesses can be targeted. Additionally, the future is bright as more persons access education and training. This is particularly crucial for females. The more educated females a nation possesses the more educated the population will become and there will be a reduction in early pregnancies. The more educated the population the greater the pool of human resources and skill needed to meet industry needs. Putting all of these possibilities together will guarantee sustainable economic development. PATH is a worthy social program but it cannot be limited to increased access to health care and increased attendance to school. It must be driven by a long term outcome of sustainable growth and development.

Bibliography

Augustine, *Confessions Books 1-X111,* Trans by F. J. Sheed, Cambridge: Hackett Publishing, 1992.
Buckner, John, Henry, *The Moravians in Jamaica*, London, 1854.
Durkeim, Emile, *The Elementary Forms of Religious Life*, London: George Allen & Unwin Ltd., 1915.
Hastings, S. U. and MacLeavy B. L. *Seedtime and Harvest: A Brief History of the Moravian Church in Jamaica, 1754-1979,* Bridgetown, Cedar Press, 1979.
Kairos Theologians: *Kairos Document: A Challenge to the Churches*, William B. Eerdmans Publishing Company, 1986.
Kelly, J. N. D., *Oxford Dictionary of the Popes*. Oxford: Oxford University Press, 1986.
Kung, Hans, et al, *Toward Vatican III: The Work that Needs to be Done*, Michigan, Seabury Press, 1978.
McGrath, Alister E, *Reformation Thought: An Introduction,* 3rd ed, London: Blackwell, 2000.
Nelson, James, *Embodiment: An Approach to Sexuality and Christian Theology*, Minneapolis, MN: Augsburg Publishing House, 1978.
Newman, John Henry, *An Essay on the Development of Christian Doctrine*, London: Longman, Green, and Co, 1909.
Philip Sherrard, *Christianity and Eros: Essays on the Theme of Sexual Love,* Limni, Greece, Denise Harvey, 2002.
The Holy Bible: New Revised Standard Version. Oxford: Oxford University Press, 1998.
Wallace, Jeff, *Darwin: The Origin of Species,* Ware, UK: Wordsworth, 1998.
Williams, Lewin, *Caribbean Theology,* Bern: Peter Lang Publishing, 1994.
UWI: Statistical Review Academic Year 2000/2001, Kingston: University of the West Indies Press, 2001.

www.ingramcontent.com/pod-product-compliance
Lightning Source LLC
Chambersburg PA
CBHW020750230426

43665CB00009B/560